Finish STRONG

The Veteran Teacher's Guide to Staying Happy, Healthy, and Highly Effective

TOM HIERCK | ALEX KAJITANI

Foreword by William M. Ferriter

Solution Tree | Press

a division of Solution Tree

555 North Morton Street
Bloomington, IN 47404
800.733.6786 (toll free) / 812.336.7700
FAX: 812.336.7790

email: info@SolutionTree.com

SolutionTree.com

Visit **go.SolutionTree.com/teacherefficacy** to download the free reproducibles in this book.

Printed in the United States of America

FSC
www.fsc.org
MIX
Paper | Supporting responsible forestry
FSC® C008955

Library of Congress Cataloging-in-Publication Data

Names: Hierck, Tom, 1960- author | Kajitani, Alex author

Title: Finish strong : the veteran teacher's guide to staying happy, healthy, and highly effective / Tom Hierck, Alex Kajitani.

Description: Bloomington, IN : Solution Tree Press, [2027] | Includes bibliographical references and index.

Identifiers: LCCN 2026005672 (print) | LCCN 2026005673 (ebook) | ISBN 9798893741131 paperback | ISBN 9798893741148 ebook

Subjects: LCSH: Motivation in education | Teachers--Social conditions | Effective teaching | Teacher-student relationships | Teachers--Professional relationships | Teachers--Job satisfaction

Classification: LCC LB1065 .H52 2027 (print) | LCC LB1065 (ebook)

LC record available at https://lccn.loc.gov/2026005672

LC ebook record available at https://lccn.loc.gov/2026005673

Acknowledgments

I'm not unaware, as I work through my forty-third year as an educator, that I'm approaching the twilight of my career. What I hope is to ensure that I do, indeed, finish strong! Preparing this manuscript and watching colleagues who have done just that (or are also in the process of doing that) remind me of what an honor and privilege it is to be an educator. I also am abundantly aware that being an educator has never been a solo act. I have benefited from the wisdom and support of colleagues in every role that defines a school community. This book is dedicated to those myriad individuals who made contributions large and small to my career. It also goes without saying that my family has been the strongest support and guidance I have received. You don't get to forty-three years without an incredible amount of patience, love, and encouragement to keep growing so you can finish strong. Thanks to my wife of forty-five years, Ingrid; my three kids, Kristin (and Ben), David, and Shannon (all working in education); and my six grandchildren, Bella, Leah, Liam, Kaiden, Wren, and Bodhi for your support. This book and the context would not have been possible without you. —Tom

My deepest thanks to the ones who have kept me going throughout an amazing career as an educator, in all its phases: my children, who've endured and laughed along at a lifetime of stories from the classroom; my wife, who has seen me through countless rainbows and rough days; and my teaching colleagues and friends, especially Martin, who make the pursuit of being a lifelong teacher even more meaningful and fun. —Alex

Solution Tree Press would like to thank the following reviewers:

Doug Gee
Educational Consultant and Associate
Solution Tree
Ankeny, Iowa

Teresa Kinley
Senior School English Teacher
Calgary, Alberta, Canada

Amy Kochensparger
Biology, AP Biology, and CCP Anatomy Teacher, Science Department Chair
Eaton High School
Eaton, Ohio

Erin Kruckenberg
Fifth-Grade Teacher
Jefferson Elementary School
Harvard, Illinois

Craig Mah
District Principal (Retired)
Coquitlam School District
British Columbia, Canada

Janet Nuzzie
Intervention Specialist, K–12 Mathematics
Pasadena Independent School District
Pasadena, Texas

Nancy Petolick
Mathematics and Reading Interventionist, Instructional Coach
Denton Independent School District
Denton, Texas

Laura Quillen
Principal (Retired)
Fairview Elementary School
Rogers, Arkansas

Tanya Rogers
Former District Principal of Early Learning and Childcare
School District No. 73 (Kamloops-Thompson)
Kamloops, British Columbia, Canada

Visit **go.SolutionTree.com/teacherefficacy** to download the free reproducibles in this book.

Table of Contents

Reproducibles are in italics.

Chapter 7

About the Authors

Tom Hierck has been an educator since 1983 in a career that has spanned all grade levels and many roles in public education. His experiences as a teacher, an administrator, a district leader, a Department of Education project leader, and an executive director have provided a unique context for his education philosophy.

Tom is a compelling presenter, infusing his message of hope with strategies culled from the real world. He understands that educators face unprecedented challenges and knows which strategies will best serve learning communities. Tom has presented to schools and districts across North America with a message of celebration for educators seeking to make a difference in the lives of students. His dynamic presentations explore the importance of positive learning environments and the role of assessment to improve student learning. His belief that every student is a success story waiting to be told has led him to work with teachers and administrators to create positive school cultures and build effective relationships that facilitate learning for all students.

His most recent books include *Trauma-Sensitive Instruction: Creating a Safe and Predictable Classroom Environment*; *Trauma-Sensitive Leadership: Creating a Safe and Predictable School Environment* (both coauthored with John F. Eller); *You're a Teacher Now! What's Next?* (coauthored with Alex Kajitani); and *You're a Principal Now! What's Next?* (coauthored with Alex Kajitani, Shan Jorgenson-Adam, and Rita Marler).

To learn more about Tom's work, visit his website (www.tomhierck.com) or follow @thierck on X or Tom Hierck on Facebook.

In 2003, **Alex Kajitani** was a struggling new teacher in one of California's lowest income neighborhoods. His middle school students seemed unmotivated, unengaged, and uninterested in the mathematics he was teaching. Demoralized and desperate, he set out on a journey to turn his class—and his life—around.

Today, Alex holds the title of 2009 California Teacher of the Year, and he was a top-four finalist for National Teacher of the Year. He is lauded for his innovation and real talk as a teacher and leader and is also known around the world as The Rappin' Mathematician™.

Alex's journey from frustrated new teacher to White House honoree is one he now shares with educators across the United States. He tells refreshingly honest stories of what it truly means to connect with students and colleagues and interweaves these stories with proven strategies that educators can implement the very next day to make an immediate impact.

A highly sought-after speaker and a top authority on student engagement, relationship building, and teacher leadership, Alex is the author and coauthor of several books, including *Owning It: Proven Strategies to Ace and Embrace Teaching*, which the U.S. Department of Education named recommended reading; *You're a Teacher Now! What's Next?*, which new teachers widely use to be highly effective in their first years; and *You're a Principal Now! What's Next?*, which new administrators widely use to be highly effective in their first years. He is also an expert on teaching online; he is the author of *101 Tips for Teaching Online*, and his virtual programs and videos are used around the world. Alex has a popular TEDx Talk and was featured on CBS Evening News, where Katie Couric exclaimed, "I *love* that guy!" And you will, too! Visit www.alexkajitani.com to learn more about his work.

To book Tom Hierck or Alex Kajitani for professional development, contact pd@SolutionTree.com.

Foreword

by William M. Ferriter

I'll never forget walking out of my classroom for the final time. After twenty-nine years of teaching—a profession that had always been loud and vibrant and full of energy and joy for me—I spent a few final moments quietly boxing up the last of the farewell letters my students and colleagues had written, and I headed for the exit alone.

When I turned the corner into the main hallway, I bumped into Will, a student I was deeply connected to. He said, "I had my dad bring me back, Mr. Ferriter. I wanted to say goodbye to you one more time."

Tears came instantly. In that moment, I realized I would never again have those simple, extraordinary interactions that defined my career. I would never watch a student succeed because of my efforts; I would never build relationships and then use those relationships to push students further than they ever thought they could go; and I'd never be the person whom a student remembered long after they had left school. The sense of loss was, and still is, overwhelming. Teaching was all I ever wanted to do and was all I had done for nearly three decades.

For years, I thought of my career as an act of service, a gift I was giving to my students and my community. But standing there crying in front of Will, I understood the truth: Teaching had been *a gift given to me*. My students and my community had shaped me just as much as I had shaped them.

And I wasn't prepared to say goodbye.

That's interesting, isn't it?

After all, most of us enter the classroom through teacher preparation programs, and we spend countless hours in professional development sessions designed to better prepare us for the challenges of classrooms. We spend our entire lives learning—about students, about teaching, about our content, and about our curricula—and yet when we reach the end of our careers, we are anything but prepared.

When I was starting out, the shelves were full of books for new teachers. Anyone else read *The First Days of School: How to Be an Effective Teacher* (Wong & Wong, 1998) or *The Essential 55: An Award-Winning Educator's Rules for Discovering the Successful Student in Every Child* (Clark, 2003)?

When I looked around at my colleagues in later years, I saw them reading books and attending workshops that targeted principals or aspiring administrators. But for guys like me? The teachers who choose to make a full career of teaching actual students in actual classrooms?

Silence.

I can't help but wonder if that silence exists because so few of our colleagues actually make it to the end of their careers in the classroom. The numbers are sobering: Teachers continue to leave the profession at alarming rates, and many who remain eventually step into other roles, seeking the kinds of challenges, opportunities, or authority that classroom teaching rarely offers (Podolsky, Kini, Bishop, & Darling-Hammond, 2016). For those of us who stay until the retirement clock runs down, there has never been much of a road map. We have always invented our own ways to stay motivated, connected, and effective.

That's why *Finish Strong* matters so much. It's the book I wish I had as I navigated the later stages of my career. It affirms the experience of the veteran teacher, acknowledges the challenges of staying energized when you've seen it all before, and offers practical wisdom about building relationships, working with younger colleagues, and preparing for life after the final bell. It's equal parts road map, pep talk, and reminder that the work we do—right up to the last day—matters more than we sometimes realize.

But it's more than just a source of advice. The opportunities for readers to reflect that are built into each chapter may be just as valuable as the information shared by the authors, because those opportunities invite you to pause, remember, and celebrate the work you have already done. In many ways, those moments of looking back are reminders that a career in teaching is worth honoring in its entirety. It's a profession served with meaning.

If I had had this book during my final decade in the classroom, I would have returned to it often—not because I didn't know how to teach but because I needed a voice reminding me that finishing strong is about more than hanging on. It's about continuing to grow and contribute and appreciating the unique privilege of being a teacher until the very end.

For those of you still in the classroom, whether you've got a year left or ten, this book is for you. Let it be the guide that many of us never had.

Introduction

It was not our idea to write this book. We had just finished keynoting a back-to-school convocation outside of Seattle, Washington, where we spent some time talking about a book we wrote for new teachers: *You're a Teacher Now! What's Next?* (Hierck & Kajitani, 2024).

A woman approached us and said, "I've been teaching for twenty-five years. I have about five more years left, and it's really hard to stay motivated—especially when I know I'll be out of here in a few more years. Where's the book for me and the rest of us who aren't new teachers, never went into administration, and still want to keep teaching strong until our very last day?"

We knew in that instant that we had to write this book.

Teaching can be very difficult. Each school year, we welcome new students, work alongside new colleagues, align ourselves with new programs and initiatives, and much more, all while we try new strategies to teach content we have (and haven't) taught before. It takes a while to get good at it. It can take even longer to *feel* like we're any good at it. And while all of this is happening, we also have our own lives outside of our schools and classrooms that need attention.

Making it past the first two years is quite a feat. Making it past the first five years means you've outlasted a large percentage of those you started with. (We save all the statistics for later in this book.) And getting to the point, making it a decade or more, when you are considered a veteran teacher—that is simply amazing.

And here you are, in all of your amazingness, looking ahead at the teaching you still have left to do and, at the same time, reflecting on all the work you've put in. And you're doing this while you're also starting to think about what your life might look like if you weren't doing the work each day (but still being committed to it while you are).

This is the book for you.

As the title suggests, *Finish Strong* is a book that will help you, as a veteran teacher, spend the final part of your teaching career (whether that's the last ten years or the last ten months) staying highly effective in the classroom while feeling healthy and happy, both inside and outside of it.

Why You Need This Book

There are many reasons veteran teachers decide to retire. They may have reached their full Social Security investment. They may have health or caregiving issues. They may be burned out. Research indicates two main factors that predict whether someone over fifty years old will consider retiring (Kreuzfeld & Seibt, 2024).

1. The ability to do their work (related to mental and physical demands, health, and existing resources)
2. Psychosocial work stress (related to an imbalance between effort and reward)

The timing of our individual retirement choices varies as well. Almost half of teachers in one poll were planning to retire early (Kreuzfeld & Seibt, 2024). On the other hand, "more Canadians than ever are taking their time transitioning out of the workforce. In fact, the average retirement age hit 65.4 in 2023—the highest in over 40 years" (Mohammed, 2025). Then, there are a growing number of people being forced into so-called involuntary retirement due to factors such as job losses, health crises, and caregiving demands. Nearly a third of older workers are in involuntary retirement according to one research review (MacLean et al., 2025).

Whatever brings you to the end of your teaching career—and whenever that time may come—this book helps you be as prepared, intentional, and empowered as possible. And until that time comes, this book offers you support and strategies to make the most of your time now, as a committed veteran teacher, with no regrets.

You can read this book solo or invite fellow veteran teachers to read along so you can plan and strategize together.

How This Book Is Organized

We (educators) all have our unique journeys, so we (Tom and Alex) decided to organize this book as a journey, supporting you through this final and important stage. The chapters break down this way.

In chapter 1, we acknowledge where you are and help you identify where you are headed. This chapter also helps you take an inventory of the time, energy, and effort that you have already put into your teaching career, as well as identify and collect the assets that have made your work have measurable impact.

In chapter 2, we take what you already know about the importance of building strong relationships and look deeper at what relationships are like at this stage of your career, what types of relationships veteran teachers need the most, and how to build on, strengthen, and preserve those relationships. It also gives practical advice for teachers to consider regarding relationships they can begin to form now that will benefit them when they retire.

In chapter 3, we discuss working with younger colleagues and address how, as a veteran teacher, it isn't always easy when a young, fresh-faced teacher shows up in the next room, filled with "new" ideas that you've already tried, or when the new principal, who is younger by a generation or two, tells you how they're going to "fix" the school that you've dedicated so much of your life to. This chapter also gives you practical, implementable advice on how to effectively communicate with, mentor (when needed), and even learn a new thing or two from a younger colleague.

In chapter 4, we lay out what many people who work in schools know but rarely discuss: Often, the most sought-after leaders at a school are not those with the official title or office. Nobody knows a school's unofficial structure and hierarchy better than the veteran teachers, who have been in the profession for a while. This chapter dives into this mostly unspoken aspect of school structure and the ways veteran teachers can use it to help themselves, their students, and their colleagues thrive.

In chapter 5, we explore one of the most rewarding aspects of teaching: sharing knowledge with others. Most often, we share our knowledge with students; however, sharing with colleagues, both in our schools as well as within the education profession, can be deeply gratifying—and sometimes there are financial rewards as well! This chapter helps veteran teachers identify what knowledge they've learned over their many years in the profession that they can contribute, as well as where and how to share it.

In chapter 6, we acknowledge that while we tell our students never to be afraid to ask for help, it's something we often avoid when we're the ones who need the help. This chapter outlines several situations and offers advice, based on real experiences, for situations where veteran teachers might need to ask for support. The chapter also goes deeper into how they can express appreciation, both proactively and reactively, to build a truly collaborative culture where everyone thrives.

Finally, in chapter 7, we lay out the most important considerations and decisions that a veteran teacher needs to make as they prepare for retirement. From figuring out money and benefits to how involved to stay in the education world, this chapter draws on the experiences and guidance of experts who have been there.

Throughout the book, we provide Reflections on the Journey narratives to share our experiences and those of colleagues who have been where you are. We share these reflections so you know that while your experiences and the perspective you've gained may be unique to you, you are not alone on this journey.

Speaking of your journey, we also include Your Turn reflection questions in each chapter. Take some time, using the space provided with these questions, to record your thoughts, memories, and reflections. Take stock of all you've learned about your career and life along the way, and better understand the spaces where you've been, where you are now, and, of course, where you're headed.

Finally, throughout each chapter, we also include several Strategies for Success boxes—based on real stories from others who've undertaken this journey—so that you can learn from others' experiences and use them to guide the work you are doing.

Here's to getting started so you can *finish strong*.

CHAPTER 1

Acknowledging Where You Are (and How Far You've Come)

There are a lot of books, workshops, and how-to videos out there for new teachers. You probably have read a lot of those books, participated in a lot of those workshops, and watched many of those videos—although depending on when you began your teaching career, you might have used a machine that included a rewind button to watch them!

Eventually, you moved beyond being referred to as a *new teacher*, and while you might not exactly have started to feel like an expert, things started to feel like they were falling into place. Not every year was perfect (or even great), but there were some topics you developed a comfort level for—ideas and strategies that you saw your colleagues using—and you adapted them to make them your own. Even some of the materials and supplies in your classroom were things you could use year after year.

Students came and went. Some even came back to visit and say hello, and some had siblings you got to teach in subsequent years.

Colleagues came and went. (Perhaps you were the colleague who came and went.) Some of them became friends. (And, if we're being honest, some of them made you roll your eyes.)

Administrators came and went. Some of them made your school and your work better. Some of them set things back a bit, but they were all trying their best.

With each passing year, you had your own comings and goings. Sometimes, personal issues outside of school made their way into your classroom. Sometimes, classroom events followed you home. The results ranged from telling funny dinnertime stories to crying about a student's safety while trying to sleep.

Yet, as we said before, here you are, still looking ahead at the teaching you still have left to do and, at the same time, reflecting on all the work you've put in—all while you're also starting to think about what your life might look like if you weren't doing the work each day. It's a worthy time for considering a broader perspective of your own *whys* and *hows*. With such reflection, you can move to this final stage of teaching with intention, focus, and an eye on what's most important for you to do and to leave behind.

This chapter explores the following topics to help you recognize, celebrate, and reflect on.

- The reasons you became a teacher (and stayed)
- The stages of (and changes during) a teaching career

Throughout this chapter, we hope you'll take some time to fill in some of the Your Turn spaces left open for you, for yours is a journey that only you can truly and deeply reflect on!

The Reasons You Became a Teacher (and Stayed)

There are a lot of reasons people become teachers. For some, it's a calling—something they knew they would do from a very young age. For others, it's something they were willing to try for a few years, and a few years later, they were still there. Others just needed a job. Regardless of the circumstances that led you to become a teacher, you chose a profession unlike so many others. It's a profession with a very difficult-to-measure bottom line. It's a profession that is not exactly known for its great pay, and it's a profession that the general public thinks has summers off. It's also a profession that challenges us every single day, giving us the deepest insight into what adults will one day look back on as a transformative part of their childhood. It's work that empowers us to see that we truly make a difference in the lives of so many.

We all have had teachers who had a tremendous impact on our lives—teachers who said things that will be forever etched in our memories (sometimes good things, and sometimes not-so-good things). Countless people became educators because of a great teacher they had. (And sometimes, they became the teacher they needed instead of those they had.)

After taking that first teaching job, most of us then learned that *becoming* a teacher was one thing, and *being* a teacher was another! That first day, first week, and first year were a lot different from what we thought they were going to be. And for some reason, or maybe for several reasons, we stayed. We came back for a second day, then a second week, and eventually a second year. Then a third. And at some point, we looked around the staff meeting and realized we weren't a new teacher anymore. Some people might have even started referring to us as a *veteran* teacher.

So before we move forward, take a moment to reflect on that first stage of your teaching journey: becoming a teacher. In all the years since, you may have forgotten some of your reasons for becoming an educator, your visions of being a teacher, and your thoughts about your early experiences. Remembering them can help you decide how you want to shape this final stage of your teaching career.

Your Turn

Why did you become a teacher?

What were some of the biggest challenges in your first few years?

What made you come back after your first year of teaching?

Reflections on the Journey: Turn a Rocky Road Into . . . Rocky Road

It was my first day of teaching English in inner-city Los Angeles, and I was crushing it! My khakis were ironed, I greeted my students with a big smile at the door, and all I could think was, "I was born for this!" I went home that day knowing that I had found my calling.

And then, the third week of school rolled around.

I suddenly realized the honeymoon was over. One of my students, Ramona, walked in with quite the attitude. Others were slap boxing each other as they entered the classroom. And were those kids playing dominoes in the back of the room? It was pretty clear that I'd lost all control. The harder I tried to regain that control, the more exhausted I got. By the time I got home, I was completely defeated.

I sought comfort the only place I knew: ice cream. That ice cream became my solace. Each night, it healed my teacher wounds. And it became the glue that held me together. Over twenty years later, I still return to this tried-and-true strategy (albeit quite a bit less often). Always have something in the freezer you can fall back on (A. Sitomer, personal communication, October 17, 2025).

—Alan Sitomer
High school teacher

The Stages of (and Changes During) a Teaching Career

As we acknowledged, not every teacher is on the same career journey. In fact, it's tough to find two teachers who are on the exact same trajectory! Whatever the trajectory, here's a truth we've all come to know: *Some years are better than others.* Having a great third year of teaching doesn't necessarily mean that we are going to have an even better fourth year. And, as many of us know, having a rough first year doesn't mean they are all going to be that way. Students change, neighborhoods change, and we change from year to year.

That said, education professor and researcher Christopher Day (2012) offers well-documented stages that teachers experience throughout their careers. Note that we all come to teaching at different ages and stages of our lives. Some of us might not have put in twenty-plus years but are still looking toward the end of our teaching career, so the big-picture feelings and stages that Day (2012) shares are worth looking at.

- **Years 0–3:** In their early years, teachers are still building confidence and learning to manage their classrooms as well as workload demands, which can be overwhelming. They also begin to shape their professional identity as teachers.
- **Years 4–7:** Teachers are continuing to build and sustain their sense of identity, self-efficacy, and effectiveness. At the same time, they become more aware of the many facets of the teaching profession and work with different colleagues and administrators with different leadership styles.

They may struggle to remain resilient and engaged in the face of a heavy workload or a lack of support during this period.

- **Years 8–15:** Teachers' roles and identities are likely to change. Major life experiences, such as becoming a parent, can deeply affect work balance and personal life. Some may also begin to question whether they are on the best career path, or they may feel that they are not growing professionally and have perhaps hit a plateau.
- **Years 16–23:** This can be a time of significant personal responsibilities, when the challenges of parenting (as well as caring for one's own parents) and other family issues (such as divorce) can be intense and lead to lower motivation and professional commitment. Career stagnation can make this time even more challenging. However, teachers who have more opportunities or see positive results from their work are more likely to feel motivated and engaged.
- **Years 24–30:** Teachers in this stage are usually committed to staying in the profession until retirement. They either have strong, sustained motivation during their last few years in the classroom or feel lukewarm about their careers at this point. Many teachers in this category have built up a wealth of experience and skill. At the same time, health and energy issues can lead to lower morale.
- **Years 31 and up:** Retirement is nigh. Many teachers either stay enthusiastic and committed or feel tired and trapped. Whichever you are, this is the right book for you, so keep reading.

Of course, all of these stages aren't necessarily linear or happen according to this timeline. According to Day (2012), "Teachers will move backwards and forwards within and between phases during their working lives for all kinds of reasons concerning personal history, psychological, social, and systemic change factors" (p. 14). In addition to a general progression throughout our careers, we contend with our changing profession (and students) and our changing selves.

Our Changing Profession (and Students)

As teachers, we strive to manage as much as we can inside our classrooms. While we quickly learn that we can't control everything, that doesn't stop us from constantly rethinking, reworking, and relearning what we might do to make our lessons land a little better, our classrooms run more effectively, or our students engage more fully. And yet, there is one thing we have almost no control over: the students who enter our classes each day and everything they are experiencing when they are away from school. While the world we create inside our classrooms is the result of our many years of experience, the world that exists outside of them is very difficult to stay on top of, especially as the age gap between us and our students grows.

According to Sam Altman, the CEO of OpenAI, "Each technological revolution has gotten faster, and this will be the fastest by far" (as cited in Jackson, 2024). As teachers, we see this firsthand in the students who enter our classrooms each school year. Each year, the group of students that enters our classrooms can be vastly different from the group a year before. They bring with them the latest technology, hum the latest lyrics, and shape themselves by the latest who's who of influential characters. All of these and more have a deep impact on how students think, interact, and learn. And still, we are expected to guide them in mastering the curriculum while they learn to navigate the school culture and the world around them. As our students change, so must our profession.

Just as our students change, so, too, must our schools to reflect the charges they serve. But even beyond our students, politicians and policymakers impact the standards we teach, the tests we administer, and the funds our schools receive. The tools we use to teach have also changed dramatically. Many of us started with things that didn't need to be plugged in (like mimeograph machines), then advanced to things that need to be plugged in (like overheads), and then circled back to things that don't need to be plugged in (like tablets). (Sure, they need to be plugged in to recharge, but you get the point.)

Yet amid it all, the central role of the teacher has not changed, nor has the profession itself. Every day, billions of students across the world arrive in classrooms, asking some version of the question "Whatcha got for me today?" And every day, the teaching profession sends those same students home a little older, a little smarter, and a little more aware of the world around them. And some even go on to be teachers themselves—perhaps the greatest testament to the work we do.

Your Turn

What does change mean to you?

Our Changing Selves

Just as our students and the educational landscape change, so do we. None of us is the same person that we were when we first started teaching. For some of us, idealism gave way to the hard-hitting reality that the job was way more difficult than we had envisioned, and we might have even had several bouts of wondering whether what we were doing was having any impact at all. (It most definitely was. Sometimes, it's just hard to see that impact each day.)

Simply put, the teacher that we started out as is not necessarily the teacher that we are today. As each school year passed, some of us got married (and remarried), some of us had children, some of us built new friendships, and some of us lost loved ones (some of whom were, unfortunately, students and colleagues). We may have struggled with health issues, both physical and emotional. (It is grueling to teach all day after throwing your back out.) Political, economic, and social forces served as a huge wake-up call, sometimes empowering us and other times leaving us feeling distraught and defeated.

And yet, we taught on. Just as the raging rapids of a river smooth the stones within it over time, the challenges we faced molded us, strengthened us, and helped us evolve into the teacher that we are today.

Reflections on the Journey: Entering Class on the Morning of 9/11

It was my first month of teaching. On my drive to work, news of the planes striking the Twin Towers in New York City came from the radio. Having arrived to my classroom but still in disbelief, I turned on our television as students began trickling in. They had heard about it as well. With thirty minutes left before first period, I had to quickly figure out what was happening and how to explain it to a room of confused middle school students.

I began creating a to-do list in my mind.

- **Step 1:** Ditch that lesson plan you were going to teach this morning.
- **Step 2:** Go get permission from the principal to address it with your class.
- **Step 3:** *(Eeeek—that's the bell.)* Get outside your door and greet your students as they walk in. Figure out the rest as you greet them.

I don't remember much of what else happened that day. I know that the students were scared (as was I and pretty much everyone else I knew). But what I do know is that I drove home that afternoon knowing that I had just passed my first true test as a teacher during what would be for many of these students the first world event they would remember experiencing. I was emotionally there for my students, explaining what was happening, reassuring them that they were safe (even though I didn't know if they were) and that I'd see them the next day. It was an experience that I would draw on during all my years of teaching.

—Alex Kajitani

Your Turn

What have been some of the major events that have impacted and shaped you throughout your teaching career?

Personal events:

National and world events:

Final Thoughts

As teachers, we are constantly looking forward. As we prepare our students for their futures, we look forward to the next lesson, the next test, and the next semester or year. (And yes, it's OK to say we look forward to the next vacation!) Many of us reading this book are beginning to look forward to something new: the last few chapters of our teaching careers and even what our post-teaching lives might look like (or what we want them to look like). The remainder of this book will help you connect, reconnect, and plan as you move ahead, all while doing what you can to stay healthy, happy, and highly effective.

We hope you've taken some time throughout this chapter to really think about why you became a teacher and why you've stayed all these years. We hope you've identified how your students, your school, and you yourself have changed, grown, and evolved. Certainly, the teacher you were when you started is not the same teacher that you are today, and certainly that evolution will continue in the years to come.

Regardless of which teaching stage you fall under, there have been events that have shaped you, both personally and professionally. The personal and the professional are often hard to separate because those big-impact students have shaped both in ways that we can never undo.

CHAPTER 2

Building, Maintaining, and Reflecting on Relationships

As teachers, we've spent our careers building relationships. Since that first bell rang on our very first day, we've been forming relationships with our students and their families, our colleagues, and the content we teach. Those connections continue long after the final bell rings on the very last day on the job. Consider this:

> Healthy work relationships facilitate greater learning and knowledge sharing, improve retention and engagement, and increase innovation and performance.
> On an individual level, people who have a sense of belonging at work [are] more likely to thrive in their jobs than those who [feel they] are [just marking time]. (Berkeley Executive Education, n.d.)

Moreover, they approach their final years or months with energy and enthusiasm rather than a resignation characterized by just putting another *X* on the calendar as they count down to their final day.

For most of us educators, the quality of our relationships has a tremendous impact on our overall happiness as teachers (at every stage of our career), and those relationships will also, in large part, determine the quality of our post-teaching lives. Dan Dalgaard is a former colleague who had a remarkable thirty-three-year career, where he continually inspired his students until the day he retired. When asked what kept him going all those years, he remarked on the importance of the team of adults he worked with, stating that his colleagues helped him "find a place where [he] belonged, while doing work worth doing" (D. Dalgaard, personal communication, May 21, 2025).

There are numerous benefits to continuing to form strong, caring, positive relationships with students and colleagues. Research and personal experience bear out that positive relationships help you weather the storm on challenging days and reflect positively on a career well enjoyed when you have delivered the final lesson. When a survey given to approximately seven-hundred teachers asked which factors play the biggest role in keeping teachers in the profession, a "love for students" was the answer most pointed to (Loewus, 2021).

Interestingly, the study also finds that retirement benefits and a love for the subjects they teach were also frequent answers. While "love for students" is probably an obvious answer for most of us, acknowledging that retirement benefits are also important is critical to recognizing that we can be at a point in our careers where we can have one eye on the work we are doing and the other on the future.

Thus, this chapter focuses on the following topics.

- Remembering those who made a big impact on us
- Building your postretirement community

As with the previous chapter, we hope you take some time to fill in some of the spaces left open for you—for yours is a journey that only *you* can truly and deeply reflect on.

Remembering Those Who Made a Big Impact on Us

We all instinctively know that strong relationships are critically important throughout our lives, especially in the work that we do as teachers. Primary among those are the relationships educators make with the closest connections they have in their classrooms and schools: students and colleagues. As you reflect on those two key groups, what can you recall as significant or even career defining? More importantly, why does that resonate with you today as you start to look at the homestretch of your career?

Students

Your teaching career has allowed hundreds (and possibly thousands) of students to benefit from your connection building with them and has played a significant part in the successes they experienced in school and in their lives beyond. This is never more apparent than when a former student drops in and reflects positively on their time with you. Did that student refer to the brilliant, well-organized lesson that you delivered as what they remember the most? Probably not. More likely, they are coming back to say hello because of how you made them feel—how they felt seen and valued by you. As Tom likes to share, "I've never had a student come back and say they were struggling in life, right up until the moment I taught them how to balance chemical equations in chemistry class."

A strong student-teacher relationship "allows students to feel confident through exploration and taking risks in their academic tasks" (Coristine, Russo, Fitzmorris, Beninato, & Rivolta, 2022). Numerous colleagues we interviewed for this book spoke about the intrinsic joy they felt from forming close relationships with students. In his book, *Significant 72: Unleashing the Power of Relationships in Today's Schools*, Greg Wolcott (2019) states, "These connections lead to greater job satisfaction, higher effectiveness, a feeling of competence, and a feeling of purpose. When the relationships and connections are good, we feel better about our abilities" (p. 6).

Some of us (like elementary teachers) have one class of students per school year. We get to know them—and, often, their families—on a more personal, day-to-day level. And some of us (like high school teachers) teach several classes per day, each filled with thirty or more students. Regardless of how many students we have or how often we see them, each school year, there are students who have a big impact on our lives and the work we do. Over several years, these students are the ones who challenge us, who delight and disappoint us, and who give the deepest meaning to the work we do. They are the big-impact students.

Big-impact students are not just the ones who are wonderful to teach. They are not necessarily the ones who reaffirm that we made the right choice to become a teacher or the ones who make us feel good about our job. Sometimes, they are the ones who make us angry, who make us question what we're doing and, equally important, *why* we're doing it. More than anything else, they are the students who create a shift in our thinking, acting, and being. They force us to grow and reevaluate why we do what we do. While we might not notice it while it's happening, they change the way we exist in and see the world. In short, they make us better (even if it takes us a while to realize it).

Take a moment to think about a few of the students who shifted your thinking, acting, and being, and fill out the following chart. And don't forget: Just as teachers have big-impact students, every student has had a few big-impact teachers, and you are most certainly one of them.

Your Turn

Think about a former student who has come back to visit you. How did you feel seeing them, and what did they say about your time together?

Who are your big-impact students? Take a moment to think about a few of those who shifted your thinking, acting, and being, and fill out the following chart.

Name and What I Remember About Them	How They Impacted Me

Colleagues

Equally important (on some days, even more important) as the relationships we have created with our students are those we have created with colleagues (Gu, 2017). Sometimes, it's because they support us unconditionally and cheer us on, even in the quiet moments when nobody else seems to be cheering. Just as big-impact students are not just the ones who are wonderful to teach, big-impact colleagues are sometimes the ones who question us incessantly and point out where we need to grow, even when it's uncomfortable and awkward. They are the ones who create a shift in our thinking, acting, and being. Ultimately, they are the ones who make us better.

It's important to note that supporting and mentoring others can often look different depending on context. Veteran teacher William (Bill) Ferriter, who wrote the fabulous foreword for this book, shares that while he isn't interested in formally mentoring colleagues, he does see that his leadership is vitally important to the colleagues he works with: "I've always seen my role in teacher leadership as raising my voice and bringing transparency to the work of teachers" (W. Ferriter, personal communication, March 17, 2025). While he does wonder whether a lack of an official mentor title impacts how his efforts with colleagues are recognized, Bill knows that his actions build and strengthen relationships in a way that has a significant impact.

The value of connecting with colleagues can't be overstated. As author Adam Grant (2013) writes in his book *Give and Take: A Revolutionary Approach to Success*, "three decades of research show that receiving support from colleagues is a robust antidote to burnout. Having a support network of teachers is huge" (p. 177). Wondering what has kept you in this job for so long? Look no further than the students you teach and the colleagues you teach with.

At times, you might have been the glue that held a team together, especially if you've remained in the same school. As you've transitioned and grown throughout your career from a rookie looking to your mentors for guidance to a veteran teacher guiding others, the relationships you build are paramount to your success and to the success of everyone you work with. Just as you've had big-impact colleagues, there's a high likelihood that for another teacher, *you* are one of their big-impact colleagues. The work you've been doing both inside and outside of the classroom is having a great impact on those around you.

Your Turn

Who are your big-impact colleagues? Take a moment to think about a few of the colleagues who shifted your thinking, acting, and being, and fill out the following chart.

Name and What I Remember About Them	How They Impacted Me

Strategies for Success: Don't Wait to Say Thank You

Take a look at the list of big-impact colleagues you just completed. Are they still teaching? If they aren't, do you know if you can still get in touch with them? If so, then don't wait until you retire to let them know what a vital role they played in your life and work. Find their contact information and let them know what you remember about them and how they shifted your thinking, acting, and being. Trust us: You'll be glad you did (even if they don't respond).

Building Your Postretirement Community

Retirement deeply impacts relationships. It is very common for retirees to miss the daily interactions with colleagues and students. What relationships will be important to you in retirement? Sure, someone from an insurance company (often at a table in the hallway after your back-to-school professional development in August) will eagerly talk about retirement services, but how does this change impact your emotional and mental health? We know that relationships are critical to both.

A study exploring the mental health status and influencing factors of retired teachers finds:

> Retired teachers should cultivate a wide range of interests and hobbies, engage in regular physical exercise, develop healthy living habits, foster a positive family atmosphere, establish harmonious family relationships, promote community cultural construction, strengthen psychological intervention, and prevent psychological diseases. (Luo, Liu, Pan, & Huang, 2024, p. 1)

While this can certainly seem like a lot (and a bit idealistic), it is achievable. Per this research, it is worth investing time in activities, your family, your health, and your colleagues. As you begin planning (even if just in your mind), remember that just as retirement impacts relationships, the inverse is also true, and your health is directly related to having a strong social circle (Ong, Mann, & Kubzansky, 2025; Pilehvari, You, & Lin, 2023).

Engage in Activities

Now is the time to follow your curiosity and pursue activities. Many retired people take up hobbies and incorporate habits suited to their individual needs (like no longer having to eat their lunch while walking to the office to quickly make more copies for their next class).

Instead of waiting until you retire, consider pursuing these things now. When you retire, you'll already be good at the activity (or at least better than you would have been if you hadn't yet started), and it will keep you excited and motivated to keep working toward retirement—so you can do more of it! You can also use it as something to talk about with students (maybe some of them have a similar interest), and you might even find that some of your colleagues take part as well, which will only serve to strengthen your current relationships.

Taking up new activities offers many benefits, including building your community, which helps improve cognitive and mental health (National Institute on Aging, 2024; Newman, 2025). Depression can rear its head during retirement, but you reduce the odds if you take part in hobbies, such as baking or cooking, or in clubs. Research shows, for instance, that attending theatrical performances and visiting museums mitigate depression in older persons (Bone et al., 2022). Participating in activities doesn't require advanced skills.

No matter how much you might miss it after you retire, never forget that you'll *always* be a teacher. Even though retired teachers aren't reporting to work each day, their skill set is always needed and valued. Volunteering is one possible application of retired teachers' skills. It is "a way individuals derive meaning through the complex interactions that make up measures of self-worth, community concept, and identity" (Cousineau & Misener, 2019, p. 61), all of which you will contend with during retirement. Plus, volunteering is good for your well-being (Matthews & Nazroo, 2021)! Many retired teachers get involved in volunteering and invest in bettering their community. Likewise, smart neighborhoods and communities should always be on the lookout for ways to incorporate retired teachers and their fabulous skill sets into improving people's lives. Consider the skill set you demonstrated as a teacher and imagine that energy and creativity going to a project that benefits your entire community. Your legacy as an educator will continue to grow!

Invest in Your Loved Ones

Teachers sacrifice a lot of family time during their careers, and they receive incredible support from their families, not only in the teaching aspects (planning, grading, conferencing with students' families) but also in the volunteer work that they do (coaching and sponsoring a myriad of activities). Families learn to adjust to these absences and time demands. But when a teacher retires, not only does the teacher go through an adjustment period but so, too, do their families. All those demands are no longer a part of their lives. Whether it's with your spouse, partner, children, extended family, or chosen family, start communicating about this now, including what you're excited and nervous about and what the next phase of your lives together might look like.

Get and Stay as Healthy as Possible (With Someone Else)

Physical health can significantly improve mental health. Don't wait until you retire to prioritize physical exercise in your daily life. Depending on the activities you pursue, exercise can also provide opportunities to connect with fellow retirees. Pairing up with someone to move increases your social contact, as well as your "commitment and accountability" (Lachman, Lipsitz, Lubben, Castaneda-Sceppa, & Jette, 2018, p. 6). This pair-up comes with a side benefit of someone else marking your progress, giving feedback, and offering assistance, which potentially increases your chance of staying with a behavior (Lachman et al., 2018).

While it might seem that taking the time to get and keep yourself healthy is time you aren't putting into the well-being of others, self-care is not selfish! In fact, consider this:

> It's OK to think of self-care as health care and ensure you are healthy and able to take on the role. Equally important—if your own mental wellness is flagging, seek help from a professional. It's not a sign of weakness and will go a long way to ensuring you can be strong in the face of these unprecedented times. (Eller & Hierck, 2021, p. 129)

A support system is pivotal to healthy behaviors (Wagner, 2017). Having a support system of like-minded colleagues is an important step, and being able to track your progress will strengthen that connection. One of the best tools we've seen is one provided by our colleague Tina H. Boogren (2025) in *180 Days of Physical Wellness for Busy Educators*. See the reproducible "Physical Wellness Accountability Partnership" (page 22) for this tool.

Keep in Touch With Colleagues Who Are Still Working

One of the many questions teachers ask as they retire is "Should I keep in touch with my colleagues who are still working?" On the one hand, the school, district, or community that retiring teachers taught in is deeply embedded in their soul, and they want to keep up with at least the occasional happenings and news. On the other hand, some want to close their classroom door on that last day and never look back after they drive away from their teacher parking spot one final time.

Ultimately, whether to keep communicating with working colleagues is a decision that is entirely up to you, but a few benefits of doing so follow.

- **You'll miss it less:** Teaching is not just what we do. Teaching is what we are. And you don't stop being a teacher just because you don't have a classroom. Keeping in touch with colleagues who are still doing the work is a great way to stay connected to students and the school community (even if it's indirectly, through your colleagues). Sometimes, all it takes is meeting a colleague for a cup of coffee one afternoon to put in perspective all that you miss—and all that you do *not* miss—about teaching.
- **You'll stay open to opportunities:** Many schools have programs that invite retired teachers and other community members to come and work with students on a limited basis. Alex's school in California, Conway Elementary School, had a program where retired community members brought in their dogs and sat with students who needed extra reading help. When it was over, the visitors all enjoyed some coffee and social time.

Staying in touch with colleagues keeps you open to these opportunities, and some of them (such as writing curriculum or tutoring) might even be an opportunity to earn a bit of additional income.

- **You'll always remember why you chose to be a teacher:** The Council of Chief State School Officers annually provides a new group of teachers with yearlong professional learning and development designed to increase their leadership skills. As the 2009 California Teacher of the Year (and a top-four finalist for National Teacher of the Year), Alex got to participate in this program during his year of service. However, the most valuable part of the program is that each year, Alex is introduced to new teachers, many of whom are still toward the beginning of their teaching careers. Despite having left the classroom, Alex was able to remain a part of a team of educators that stays connected. Although you may leave your classroom, it is possible to stay connected with active educators you have helped shape and who may soon be joining you in the world of retirement!

Your fellow teachers have traveled this journey with you up to now, and they've made it richer, less lonely, and more connected. In his application for California Teacher of the Year, Alex wrote this:

> By being teachers, and embodying the commitment that is inherent to living and working as teachers, we are inspiring, creating, and invoking in our students the pride and confidence to make this world a better place. Above all, we are doing it together.

Final Thoughts

As a veteran teacher, you are likely very similar to this book's authors in that you have, by and large, been in school your entire life. From your thirteen-year kindergarten-through-twelfth-grade experience as a student to your college days (another four or more years) to that first job many years ago, you are a *lifer*. Finishing strong is important to you based on all the relationships you have built over time, and these relationships will carry you to the very end. You'll likely still connect with former students, parents, community members, and colleagues. And you'll continue to build new relationships and strengthen current ones in the time you have left in this career.

Teaching involves strong, multifaceted relationships driven by the connections built with all the constituents we previously identified. These relationships are crucial for effective teaching and student success, with the focus on growth and development. While these deep connections have supported students and colleagues, they have also been essential to your career and your life. Your legacy resides in the variety of people you've interacted with and the positive message you've left with each one of them.

Physical Wellness Accountability Partnership

Conveying our preferences in writing can be easier than conveying them verbally, and accountability partners can use this sheet to help them accomplish that. In the two shaded cells in the first row, insert your name and your accountability partner's name. Then, work through the sheet to iron out the details of your partnership in the two blank columns. Be aware that as you work together, you both may want to revisit your preferences.

	Name: ______________	Partner: ______________
My goal		
Milestone one (mini-goal and date)		
Milestone two (mini-goal and date)		
Milestone three (mini-goal and date)		

Milestone four (mini-goal and date)		
How often I'll check in with my partner and by what method (in person, by text, by app direct message, by phone call, or other)		
How we'll track our progress (via shared document, app, verbal communication, shared notebook, or other)		
How I want to be held accountable		
What doesn't work for me		

Source: Boogren, T. H. (2025). 180 days of physical wellness for busy educators. *Solution Tree Press.*

Source for partnership information: Adapted from Hardy, B. (2019, January 17). Accountability partners are great. But "success" partners will change your life. *Accessed at https://medium.com/@benjaminhardy/accountability-partners-are-great-but-success-partners-will-change-your-life-8850ac0efa04 on March 2, 2026.*

CHAPTER 3

Working With Younger Colleagues

An odd thing happens when you stay in one profession for a long time: Some of the people around you start getting younger. At some point, the new hires seem significantly younger than you. Sometimes, this is wonderful: It's a chance to collaborate with someone closer to the age of your students and more connected to current pop culture, slang, and tech. But let's be honest: Sometimes, it can be really tough.

A new, inexperienced teacher shows up in the next room, determined to put all of what they've learned in their credential program to immediate use (and success) and seemingly uninterested in all you've learned over your many hard-earned years. Or the new hotshot administrator, branded the "turnaround principal," comes in and begins uprooting some of the programs you've been working on for years. Or the person the school district has brought in to train everyone on the newest technology talks way too fast and seems like they have very little patience for those who haven't had a mobile device in their hand since birth.

This chapter addresses both the wonderfulness and challenges of working with younger colleagues, and it gives you practical, implementable advice on how to effectively communicate with them, mentor them when needed, and even learn a thing or two from them along the way. Specifically, we look at the following topics.

- Understanding the different generations
- Working with younger teachers
- Working with younger administrators
- Staying relevant and authentic

As teachers, we work in a profession that is constantly changing. It's a job that is multifaceted and multigenerational. And while this can be very challenging at times, it can also be one of the reasons we love it.

Understanding the Different Generations

Just as there are generational gaps between teachers and students, so, too, are there generational gaps between teachers and administrators. Instead of seeing the generational gaps as something that divides us, what if we saw them as something that could bring us together and ensure the future of our profession? With each new generation that enters our profession, the industry gets a wave of new ideas, new approaches, and new ways of seeing the world. This wave mixes in with all of the waves that have come before it and creates irreversible change. (In this case, "irreversible" is not a bad thing!) Moreover, when we turn our generational differences into something we acknowledge, embrace, and celebrate, we greatly improve how we feel about the work we do.

Although exact years vary, generally, four generations work together, and a fifth generation of students is attending our schools (White, 2022). This can be an amazing opportunity for all of us. Simply naming these generational groups can begin to shed light on how we can all work better together. Here is a quick overview on the generations in our workforce. (Although we wanted to, we have not listed the generation known as the *traditionalists*, as those folks are in their eighties and likely not working.) Figure 3.1 graphically presents the generations who are our workplace colleagues.

- **Baby boomers:** Born between 1946 and 1964, baby boomers lived their formative years during the dawn of television, rock 'n' roll, the civil rights era, and the Vietnam War. Many boomers hold the institutional memory of their schools and the educational system and can add valuable insight into teaching trends that have come and gone and ways we can all apply those lessons to newer initiatives.
- **Generation X:** Born between 1965 and 1980, the Gen Xers grew up in a time that included the introduction of MTV and the personal computer, the explosion of the *Challenger* space shuttle, and the Iraq War. Unintimidated by technology and equipped with a couple of decades of experience working in schools, Gen Xers are well positioned in leadership roles, both in and out of the classroom.
- **Millennials:** Also referred to as *Generation Y* or *Next*, millennials were born between 1981 and 1996. They are now the largest group in the modern workforce. They came of age with events such as the school shootings at Columbine and Virginia Tech, the 9/11 attacks, and the dawn of the internet and the Information Age. Skilled at creating with and using

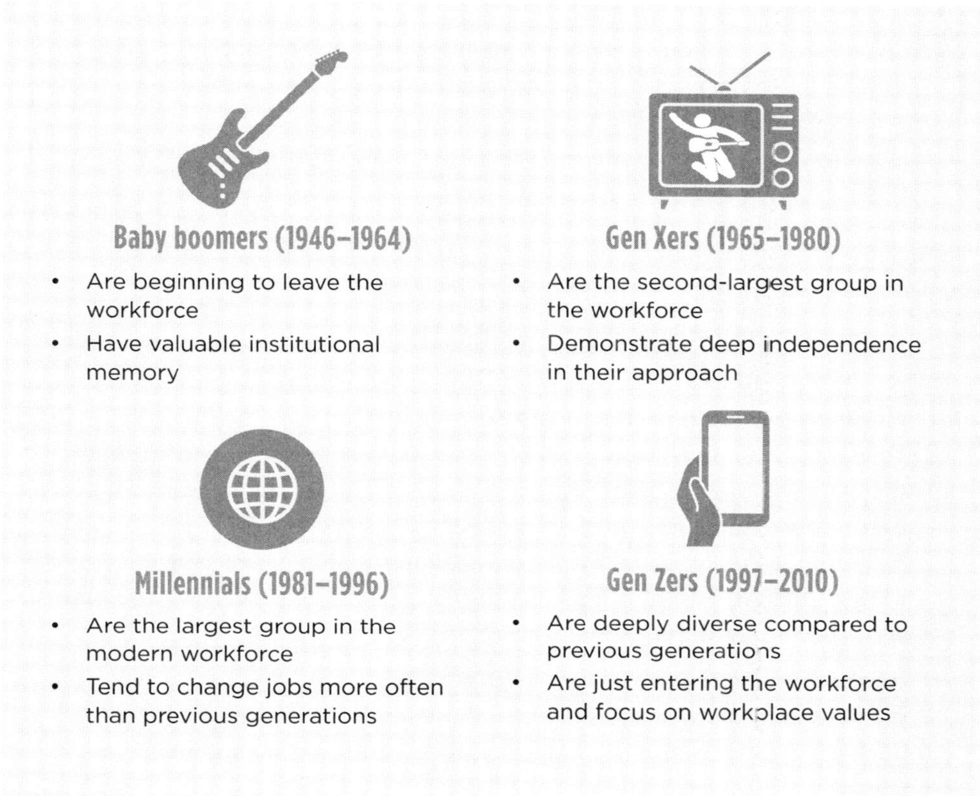

Source: Adapted from Haiilo, 2024; Lee, 2022.

FIGURE 3.1: Workplace colleagues by generation.

technology, many millennial educators are part of large engaged networks that they can tap into for creative, effective solutions to the challenges they face. Millennials are growing themselves into leadership roles, and leadership will continue to grow into them quickly!

- **Generation Z:** Born between 1997 and 2010, Gen Z is the newest generation entering our workplaces. Gen Z joins our schools and offices in a time when social media is the norm and politics are anything but usual. Many educators refer to members of this generation as *digital natives*: people who grew up in a technology-dominated world. They bring with them unprecedented experience and savvy for the digital world, entrepreneurship, and all types of diversity, which will most certainly benefit modern students and more experienced colleagues. They have great potential to lead our schools with their technological capabilities, as well as with their new ideas and the ability to implement those ideas at resounding speeds!

- **Generation Alpha:** This generation is generally defined as those born between 2011 and 2025. They are the first generation to be born entirely in the 21st century, with a still-unknown pathway to the ranks of professional educators. We look forward to the unique characteristics and style they'll bring to our world and the many contributions they'll make to education!

So the question remains: How can you, as a veteran teacher, use this knowledge to stay happy, healthy, and highly effective? We offer the following guidance.

- **Don't compare:** Acknowledging our differences is important. But don't get sucked into what your generation does "better" or the advantages the younger generations seem to come in with. Ageism works both ways. Younger people don't want to experience ageism from you any more than you want to experience ageism from them. Try to see generational differences as something that, if respected, benefits everyone in your school community. Pointing out (in a meeting, for example) that each generation brings different styles and strategies to the table and that each has strengths worth incorporating acknowledges difference in a positive way.
- **Remember that they're unsure of how to work with *you*:** Just as you see the younger generations coming into the workforce and can be a bit baffled by them, they often feel intimidated and are confused about how to work with you. They want to make a good impression on you and learn from your expertise and wisdom. What might look like occasional avoidance might just be intimidation. Being respectful and empathetic will make you more approachable and will help both you and your younger colleagues.
- **Remember that mentorships work both ways:** As someone who has been at this job for a while, you have things you can pass along to the younger generations—but avoid falling into the trap of thinking that mentorship only works one way. The younger generations have a lot to teach us as well! Being open to learning from them—and even insisting that their knowledge be part of your professional development—will put you at a great advantage, and you'll make some new friends as well.

Your Turn

Reflect on yourself, as well as your school and colleagues.

Which generation are you, and how do you align with what you read about that generation?

Which of your colleagues fit into the following generations, and how can you tell?

Baby Boomers	Gen Xers

Millennials	Gen Zers

Working With Younger Teachers

As teachers, most of our work happens with students. Most of the time (if not always), those students are a lot younger than us. The age gap between a teacher and their students is a natural and expected dynamic. The teacher brings with them years of experience, education degrees, and wisdom that they can share with future adults. But then, something weird happens: Those students become our colleagues. They're no longer children who show up to our classes each day to follow directions and learn from us. Now they're adults who show up each day to chart their own directions and teach alongside us. And they're different from us. They are at a different point in their lives and careers, they have different priorities and goals, and they see the world and ways to move forward in it through a much different lens than we do. Sure, we're all teachers, but sometimes, it seems like that's where any similarities end. The good news is that research suggests that mixed-age teams tend to perform better than teams where all educators are of the same relative age and background (Alboher, 2024).

And our success, especially as we move to wrap up our careers, depends deeply on working well with our younger colleagues. They'll be here long after we retire. Many of them will have moved into positions of school leadership (sometimes very quickly), and they can help us continue to grow and evolve.

We offer the following strategies for working with younger teachers and colleagues.

- Limit talking about the way things used to be.
- Offer help, but don't force it on them.
- Don't avoid technology.
- (Re)consider your communication style.
- Don't feel like you have to go out with them (and don't get offended if you're not invited).

Limit Talking About the Way Things Used to Be

It's OK to feel older, but you don't have to routinely bring up "the good old days" to your younger colleagues. Feeling "old" is a natural part of, well, *getting older*. Fortunately, the education profession is often one where being a bit older is seen as an advantage. Many families would rather have their child assigned to the experienced veteran teacher's class than to the energetic new one's. There's just something comforting about knowing your child is being taught by someone who has been doing it for years.

Diverse age groups working together actually can reduce ageism (Alboher, 2024), especially if you avoid the kinds of common refrains with younger colleagues, such as the following, that most often contribute to ageism.

- "That was before your time."
- "Back in my day . . ."
- "I'm too old to understand / deal with / learn that."

Offer Help, but Don't Force It on Them

Everyone needs help from time to time. Often, it is the new teachers on your campus who need the most help. Some of them are right out of college, and some switched careers midlife. It can be very frustrating to offer someone advice and watch them not follow that advice. One of the best things you can do is simply say, "I struggled with that as well. Let me know if you need help or want to talk." This leaves your newer colleague feeling supported without feeling lectured at. When they're ready to hear what you have to say, they'll come find you, and this prevents you from feeling like you gave advice that wasn't followed!

Don't Avoid Technology

It's an old refrain that the pace of technological change is accelerating. It was true for the teaching generation before you, and it's even more true of your generation of teachers. There is no sign of this acceleration slowing down anytime soon (Jackson, 2024). This is incredibly apparent in our profession. Just as humans find different and hopefully better ways to live and exist, educators are constantly seeking better ways to help students learn.

For those of us who have been teaching for decades, that also means that we have to learn alongside our students, and technology can be one of the biggest challenges for veteran teachers (Tariq, Dilawar, & Muhammad, 2019). Each year, there seems to be a new tech device, a new program, or a new "way of doing" to learn. Maybe you'll need it next year; maybe you won't. By the time you finish this book, the tech you were using when you started might already be outdated! But committing to learning as much as you can will keep you fresh, in the know, and on the cutting edge.

Then, of course, there are the trainings where we are expected to learn the new technology program or the devices that support it. The room is quickly split into those who seem to easily pick up the new technology and those who have trouble logging in. Working with younger colleagues is an opportunity to grow in new ways, especially with regard to technology. Why not empower those around us to help us grow in this area? Why not give them an opportunity to sharpen their teaching skills?

When interacting with and learning new technology, here are a few tips that can really accelerate your learning.

- **Have the person helping you put their hands in their pockets:** When helping someone with technology, it's only natural to want to grab the device and do it for them. But when someone does that to us, we become an observer rather than a participant. Physically participating in hands-on learning of new skills has been shown to produce more accurate results than merely observing (Alhajri, Hodges, Zwicker, & Virji-Babul, 2018). Putting their hands in their pockets or behind their back forces the teacher to more clearly explain what we need to learn and gives us the hands-on responsibility for learning it.
- **Give yourself fail time:** We don't expect our students to grasp everything we teach them the first time around, so why would we expect it of ourselves? Instead of trying to get it right instantaneously, give yourself fifteen minutes of fail time. Set the expectation that things won't go according to plan, other things will go wrong, and nothing will be mastered. This takes the pressure off you to learn everything you're supposed to very quickly and opens you up to getting familiar with the tech. After that fifteen minutes (or however long you need), you'll probably feel more comfortable and open to learning.

- **Embrace a growth mindset:** Sure, this might not be the most scientific statement you'll read in this book, but it's certainly true—whether we're learning how to add fractions with unlike denominators, how to execute a new dance move, or how to use the new district-approved gadget, there will be a time when you feel awkward, uncomfortable, and, well, stupid. This feeling is totally normal, natural, and—most importantly—temporary. Acknowledge it, feel it, and then move past it. You have more important things to do. Shifting from feeling ignorant to feeling curious can make all the difference.

(Re)consider Your Communication Style

Certain communication styles tend to be inextricably linked with age, as it is well documented that different generations have different communication styles. According to Nancy Collamer (2013), author of *Second-Act Careers: 50+ Ways to Profit From Your Passions During Semi-Retirement*, "Communication styles between generations tend to be different—millennials are more willing to put their personal lives out there at work, while older generations don't do that" (p. 178).

Choosing to be curious about and open to the communication styles of younger colleagues offers more possibilities for connection and collective success. For example, instead of focusing negatively on the perceived short attention span of Gen Z colleagues, we can embrace how they "value authentic and transparent communication, favoring genuine interactions," and we can learn from their digital savvy (Fitzsimmons, 2023). Furthermore, it behooves us to remember that they are closer in age to students, and we can gain creative strategies to connect with our own students by soaking in our younger colleagues' inclusive, visual, interactive, and tech-savvy ways (Fitzsimmons, 2023).

Don't Feel Like You Have to Go Out With Them (and Don't Get Offended If You're Not Invited)

Sure, we might all sit together in staff meetings, but that doesn't mean we're all going to sit together at a café. People naturally prefer to socialize with people similar to themselves (Bahns, Crandall, Gillath, & Preacher, 2017). It can be a bummer hearing younger colleagues planning a happy hour but not inviting you, but it can also be a relief! If that is something you would truly like to be a part of, act accordingly: "I could use some time decompressing after work. Would it be all right if I joined you?" They may or may not be comfortable with older colleagues joining them, but it can't hurt to ask. And don't take their response personally. If they invite you and you really *don't* want to go, it's fine to politely decline with good humor. Here's the bottom line: If you want to do it, ask. If you don't want to join, don't. You can connect in other ways.

Reflections on the Journey: "New Teachers These Days"

I will never forget my first semester of student teaching. Along with a few others in my credential program, I was placed at the local middle school, and each of us was partnered alongside an experienced teacher. We were working hard, learning from our mistakes, and feeling excited to be progressing. After our student teaching each morning, we were required to run back to our university to attend classes and discuss our experiences.

One day, as I entered the teachers' lounge to grab a snack, I heard a small group of the school's teachers mid-conversation. They were talking about us!

One of them said, "Geez, this year's student teachers are really lazy. They don't seem very interested, and after class, they just run out of here." And another replied, "When I was a student teacher, I remember having to work way harder than they do."

While I quietly slipped out of there (I wasn't confident or informed enough to speak up, and I was still trying to make a good impression), I was devastated at what I'd just heard. Over the years, I came to see this quick thing I'd overheard as a gift. Whenever I heard some of my colleagues start to complain about the "new teachers these days," I told them this story. We all had a good laugh and shifted the conversation to how we could support them.

—Alex Kajitani

Your Turn

What do you recall about your interactions with veteran teachers when you started teaching?

What are some possible generational differences or patterns you have noticed about some of the new teachers you work with?

Working With Younger Administrators

Let's be honest: There's a difference between *working with* people who are younger than you and *being told what to do* by someone who is younger than you. Sure, age should be irrelevant, but we work in a profession where age is often equated with experience. Plus, a study found that "age and length of service significantly influenced principals' pedagogical leadership practices" (Berhanu, 2025, p. 1). In education, we love to know that the people who are leading us have been alongside us, sleeves rolled up while in the trenches. So when a younger (sometimes much younger) principal moves in, it can be tough—especially when they bring with them a mandate to fix, save, or reform the school that you have devoted much of your life to. Things can get even harder when your school has seen a revolving door of administrators, and it feels like you are starting over each time the name on the office door changes.

Here's the bottom line: The more your principal (and all other school administrators) succeeds, the more you and your school succeed, and this is critically important as you move toward the latter part of your career. When your leadership team is successful, it opens up the time and energy for you to do your best work as a teacher.

Following are tips that Alex wrote about in an *Education Week* article (Kajitani, 2016) to help you proactively build a relationship with an administrator who is younger than you.

- Introduce yourself (and don't be the only one who does).
- Advocate.
- Be compassionate.

Introduce Yourself (and Don't Be the Only One Who Does)

Sure, this may seem simple or obvious, but proactively introducing yourself sends an important message to your new boss: "I'm here, I've been here, and I'm excited that you are here." When the whole staff introduces themselves, that communicates a "much different message than a group who sits in their classrooms and waits. When introducing yourself, use this opportunity to ask about the new principal's background, leadership style, and what matters most to them in a school community" (Kajitani, 2016). This small act can make a big impact.

Advocate

Both of us have had the great opportunity to travel North America and collaborate with teachers and administrators on how to effectively lead and coach at their schools. Many a teacher has had an amazing program dismantled by a new principal. It's critically important to be proactive and speak up for what matters to you. A principal forms foundational beliefs about a school in their first few years in the profession, just as teachers do, so "*don't sit back and wait for the principal to figure out what you're working on*" (Kajitani, 2016; italics added). Meet with the principal and relay what you believe is most important about your work, what has succeeded in the past, and what you would ideally like to see in the future regarding education. In other words, "you don't want your work to end up as just another line item in a principal's budget. Advocate proactively for your work" (Kajitani, 2016). You want to make sure the principal knows your face, name, and story. It can make a difference when they are tasked with choosing programs.

Be Compassionate

Leadership is a tough gig. Remember how nervous you were as a new teacher? Everyone, whether they are new to a role or new to a school, wants to be respected. You know that rare is the leader (especially a young leader) "who [doesn't] want to be a well-respected, effective leader (and yes, raise test scores—as their jobs often depend on it, to no fault of their own)" (Kajitani, 2016). As you know, most principals have classroom experience. They likely have much less experience managing people and no experience exercising buildingwide authority. After all, few leadership courses are offered to future educators, so "leadership is something they learn along the way" (Kajitani, 2016). Overall, "keep in mind that the leader they are today is not necessarily the leader they are becoming and understand that, like every great teacher, they will struggle and not always handle every decision with perfect execution and grace" (Kajitani, 2016). In these moments, how you react, as a veteran teacher, will set the tone for the rest of the school.

Compassion makes a difference to your students when they are learning from you, and it makes a difference to a young administrator who is also learning from you.

Strategies for Success: Be Respectful When Talking to Your Younger Boss

As a veteran teacher, you can set a positive tone with your new, younger boss by reframing some old, unhelpful language.

You might find yourself wanting to say something like the following.

- "That's not the way we do things."
- "I've been here way longer than you (and will probably be here after you're gone!)."
- "You really messed that one up!"

For a more productive conversation, try saying something like the following instead.

- "Up to this point, here's what we've found to be most effective." (And maybe follow it up with "and I'm open to new ideas!")
- "I've learned a lot during my years at this school. Here's what I can share."
- "How can I [or we] help you fix this?"

Staying Relevant and Authentic

As new teachers, many of us were hungry for professional development. Everything we learned seemed new, relevant, and worth a try. As the years went on, for many of us, that enthusiasm began to dissipate. Perhaps it was another training that didn't really seem like it pertained specifically to us, but we had to sit there anyway because that's what had been planned. Or perhaps it was a training that we had already been to fairly recently, and for some reason, there we were again. Or perhaps the person leading it clearly had very little experience actually doing what they were telling us we should be doing. Do any of these scenarios sound familiar?

Think about how much you grew as an educator in your first five years. Sure, you don't need Classroom Management 101 seminars and think-pair-share workshops, but why should the last five years be any different? Learning, growing, and evolving are parts of finishing strong. The students who walked into your classroom five years ago were vastly different in so many ways from the students you are teaching today, and today's students will be different from those five years from now. Staying on top of the latest teaching strategies, methods, and research will help you be highly effective, and being highly effective in your final ten years will help you stay sustained and satisfied.

As we discussed in chapter 2, you might find enjoyment and fulfillment leading professional development and sharing the lessons, stories, and strategies that you've acquired. Here are strategies for making the most of professional development as you head toward retirement.

- **Specialize:** There is a pretty good chance that any professional development session you attend in your final years is going to be highly familiar. One way to focus your mind and reap the benefits of that professional learning session is to find nuance on the topic (McDowell, 2021). Instead of just taking in the information (and possibly rejecting or being bored by it), find the specialized nuances that you can use to push and challenge your own thinking. For example, if a presenter is talking about classroom management and you're a pro at it, listen for a new tip relevant to the tech-savvy younger generations that you can incorporate to freshen things up. This way, you stay engaged in your own professional learning until the very last day.

- **Use your institutional memory:** One of your greatest advantages is having seen professional development approaches, topics, and experts come and go over the years. How has classroom management changed since you began? What about how we teach adding fractions? Or what about the way they design and structure education conferences these days? Being able to reflect on how things have changed is a surefire way to stay engaged, keep learning, and be mentally sharp as you seek patterns and evaluate.
- **Share what you've learned:** As we often like to say in teaching, "The one doing the talking is the one doing the learning." Want to make sure you keep learning and developing until your very last day? Share what you know. You've been around long enough to know what's good, what's not so good, and what teachers need the most. So whether it's simply telling a relevant story during a professional learning session or planning and delivering an entire workshop for your colleagues, sharing your expertise is a great way to stay engaged and highly effective. And you never know—your presentations might be something that people pay you to deliver once you "retire"!
- **Ask for what you need:** Veteran teachers are still interested in and open to professional development, but they have specific needs that are not always met in their schools (Aldridge & Witherspoon, 2023). What are you interested in learning about as a veteran teacher? Use what you know about advocating for yourself and your peers to request professional development on those topics. You can also talk with your veteran peers and, together, ask administrators for training most relevant for your group.

We address professional learning about technology in more depth in this chapter's Don't Avoid Technology section (page 31).

Here's the bottom line: When you hit a point where it seems difficult to learn something new, don't be shy about grabbing one of your younger colleagues and saying, "I need your expertise!" You'll not only lead by example that it's OK to ask for help, but you'll also instill in them the knowledge that they are a valued, trusted member of your school community.

Final Thoughts

As a teacher, you've been working with younger people your entire career. And as odd as it may seem, now some of those students are colleagues, sometimes even your boss!

Even though our job title is *teacher*, we all know that we've always been learning alongside and from the people we teach. Some of the most important lessons we've learned have come directly from the people who were supposed to be learning from us. And while it can be a challenge to communicate with colleagues from other generations and with other perspectives, one of the greatest gifts our profession offers is multiple opportunities for our students to learn each day from people of different ages and experience levels.

So as weird as it may be having someone significantly younger than us tell us what to do, we finish strong and learn from not only those who came before us but those who came after us as well.

CHAPTER 4

Understanding That Not Every Leader Has (or Needs) a Title

Here's something we all know but rarely talk about: Often, the most sought-after leaders at a school are not those with the official titles or offices; they are the ones the other teachers quietly go to in their times of need for advice, encouragement, or sometimes just a listening ear.

While every school has an official structure, each also has its own unofficial structure. Nobody knows that hierarchy better than the veteran teachers at that school. Perhaps you are one of the people other teachers confide in, or perhaps you aren't. Regardless, there are leadership skills that veteran teachers have developed that are especially helpful toward the end of their careers. Whether you obtained these skills through training and practice or developed them through experience and instinct, this chapter dives headfirst into those skills so that you can continue to be effective in the work that you do each day and finish strong.

We cover the following topics.

- Running effective meetings
- Connecting with your students' families
- Stopping toxic conversations in the teachers' lounge and parking lot
- Saying yes (and saying no) to all those extras
- Having difficult conversations and dealing with conflict

Running Effective Meetings

As a veteran teacher, you've sat through *a lot* of meetings, and we're going to make a big assumption that not every one of those meetings was productive, enjoyable, and worthy of your time. *Are we right?* In many (if not most) cases, the determining factor as to whether the meeting was worth everyone's time comes down to one thing: the person running the meeting.

Often, others look to veteran teachers to provide meeting guidance. Make sure the time is valuable to your colleagues and establish yourself as a leader on campus. When the person leading the meeting runs a boring meeting, they're often seen as boring. When they run a meeting that is exciting and productive, they're often seen as someone who is exciting and productive.

Here are ideas that will help you liven up any meeting, keep it on track, and make it worth everyone's time.

- **Bring some food:** Lots of people love having food at a meeting. It doesn't need to be anything fancy. Just a few pieces of fruit, good bread, or cookies can make an impact. It's hard to think about what a miserable time you're having in a meeting while you're eating a baked good, so when you feel like you need to liven up a meeting, try bringing in something for everyone to munch on. In addition, sharing some food naturally brings people together, and it can break down hierarchies and make discussions more relaxed and open.
- **Start with the question "Why are we here?":** Just as it's good teaching practice to state the objective at the beginning of a lesson, adults need to know why they've been called together (and "Because we're supposed to meet every Tuesday for an hour" is *not* a good reason). You can ask this question aloud or have someone else ask it. Or you can simply start by saying, "The purpose of this meeting is ______________." When everyone in the meeting has a clear understanding of why they're there and what you will cover, they may be more invested in participating, being productive, and (hopefully) ending on time.
- **Stay on track:** It's happened to all of us. We're in the middle of a meeting, and the conversation takes a small turn away from what we are supposed to be discussing and keeps on moving in that direction, getting further and further from why we're meeting. How can you curb this? Simply say, in a calm voice, "All right, let me get us recentered on why we're here," and move the conversation back to the intended goal. Everyone will appreciate you getting the meeting back on track, and you'll look like the kind of leader who can keep the meeting focused and productive.

- **End with the question "So, what's the plan?":** You and your team have just met for an hour. You discussed some important things, and everyone is feeling good. What often happens when the meeting ends? More often than not, everyone goes back to their classroom, throws their meeting notes on their desk, and moves on to something else. The next time they look at those notes (if they even look at them at all), they might have a hard time remembering what you talked about. To prevent this, ask what the plan is near the end of the meeting. It doesn't need to be a fifteen-point plan, but each participant should be able to articulate their next steps. Many people respond well to having a deadline. (As a popular saying goes, "If it weren't for the last minute, nothing would get done.") Then, follow up about each person's action steps during the next meeting.

Strategies for Success: Offer Sticky Notes to End the Meeting

At the end of a meeting, have each participant write their immediate next steps on a sticky note. Then, have everyone pass their notes in a circle so that everyone gets a chance to see what everyone else wrote. Once everyone gets their own note back, they can revise what they wrote for their next steps.

When everyone returns to their room, they can stick the sticky note on their desk as a reminder of what they need to do (and to hold themselves accountable to do it).

Connecting With Your Students' Families

Over the years, you've had a lot of students come through your classroom. This also means that you've had a lot of parents and guardians come through as well. There's also a strong possibility that you've had repeat parents, as you've taught siblings. A few of us have even taught students whose parents are former students! In addition, many of us have worked in schools that have experienced a demographic shift in the surrounding community, and the language, culture, and priorities of our students' families have shifted as a result. And, of course, how we communicate with parents and guardians has changed. What used to be occasional phone calls and annual conferences are now social media and texting at seemingly all hours of the day.

Whatever your own reality, you already know how critically important it is to build strong relationships with our students' parents and guardians, and you've met enough parents to know that what happens at home has a direct impact on what happens at school the next day. As a veteran teacher, you have a distinct advantage because you have years of experience interacting with your students' families. Many parents already know you, and when a situation arises, it's often not the first time you have dealt with it. Just as students change each year, so do their caregivers. (It just might not be as obvious, since you don't see them every day!)

To stay motivated and highly effective in building relationships with parents and guardians, keep the following in mind: *Everyone* has a preferred method of contact. Have you ever texted a friend and gotten no response back, only to see that they've been active on social media while you were hoping to hear from them? Or perhaps you've left more than a few voicemails asking for someone to call you, only to send them a text and get an immediate reply? Finding a parent or guardian's preferred method of contact can save you lots of time reaching out and waiting for a response. All you need to do is distribute a quick online survey or send home a quick form that parents can fill out.

Figure 4.1 offers a form for this purpose.

What is your preferred method of being contacted? Write a 1 in the box of your top preference and a 2 in the box of your second preference.

(Important note: Only provide contact methods that you are willing to do!)

☐ Text me. (Please provide a cell phone number.)

____

☐ Call me. (Please provide the best number to reach you.)

____

☐ Email me. (Please provide an email address.)

____

☐ Mail me a letter. (Please provide a mailing address.)

____

____

____

☐ Use social media. (Please provide a preferred platform and username.)

________________ ________________

Source: Kajitani, 2022, p. 72.

FIGURE 4.1: Example contact preferences email.

Visit ***go.SolutionTree.com/teacherefficacy*** *for a free reproducible version of this figure.*

As someone who has been in the profession for a while, you know that there are endless interpretations of what it means to be an involved parent. Some parents and guardians are seemingly impossible to get ahold of, while others are *highly* and *deeply* involved. Most families fall somewhere in the middle.

One of the things successful educators learn is to see students' families as teaching partners. In most cases, a parent or guardian is a child's first teacher, and it's a great idea to take advantage of their presence, when available, to help support their child's education. That doesn't mean that you need to count on adults at home to reteach your lessons, but you can encourage them to discuss at home some of the content you've taught in school, which can be very powerful.

Each week, consider sending out (using one or several methods of contact) a question of the week that parents or guardians can ask their children. The question should not require students to have been in class, but make sure it's loosely related to the content you have covered in class. For example, after teaching about fractions, send home a question that empowers the adult at home to ask, "What are all the ways we use fractions in our family?" (such as cooking and telling time). Or after teaching a lesson on art, have the adults ask, "What are some of your favorite famous pieces of art or favorite works of art that you have made?" And remember, questions work both ways. You can send students home with questions they can ask their parents or guardians in hope that those discussions will get families more aware of what students are studying.

When we see parents and guardians as people who can help our students think about and understand the content at a deeper level, we reinforce what often takes veteran teachers many years to figure out: We don't need to teach alone.

Your Turn

Think about something you are going to teach and one question the adults can ask their children, as well as a different question you can have your students ask their parents or guardians.

Something I'll teach:

One question I can ask a family to ask their child:

One question I can have my students ask their adult family members:

Stopping Toxic Conversations in the Teachers' Lounge and Parking Lot

Ask a group of veteran teachers why they went into teaching, and you'll get a lot of different reasons, but none of them will be "so that I could complain about students." Yet there seem to be those among us who do just that.

Teaching is hard—*really hard.* From time to time, we all need to vent. But how, where, and to what extent we vent are very important, not only for ourselves but for the entire profession. When a new teacher complains about students and says negative things, it's unfortunate. But when a veteran teacher does it, it's different: It's built on many years of experience and frustration. When new and mid-career teachers hear a veteran saying negative things about students, colleagues, or the profession, it sets a tone and creates a culture that can be hard to reverse. Consider this:

> At first glance, complaining seems harmless. It can even feel cathartic, like releasing the pressure valve on a boiling pot. However, experts believe chronic complaining rewires your brain for negativity. The more you complain, the more your brain strengthens neural pathways that make you prone to finding fault. . . .
> Complaining shrinks the hippocampus—an area of the brain that's critical to problem-solving and intelligent thought. (Gill, 2024)

Tune into what language you use. If you notice yourself starting sentences with "Ugh," "Can you believe . . .?" and "Why is it always . . .?" stop and take a deep breath (Gill, 2024). Then, think about how you can reframe your complaints. Can you flip the script and find a positive? (For example, consider those super-active students as an opportunity to incorporate more kinesthetic learning into your class.) Can you become a problem solver? (Instead of going to someone with a complaint, offer a suggestion that might address the issue.) You'll likely find that breaking your complaining habit will increase your enjoyment at work as well as your colleagues' respect for you.

A veteran teacher not engaging in toxic talk is pretty obvious. Often, the harder question is "How do you prevent others from doing it?" Here are strategies for shutting down toxic talk as a veteran teacher.

- **Ask a question:** You've just heard a colleague complain about a student or say something negative. Instead of agreeing or disagreeing with them (which could either validate or infuriate them), ask a question to get them explaining their thinking further. Try something like the following.
  - *"What makes you say that?"*—This question is not very combative, as it holds no judgment; it just gives the person talking some extra time to explain themselves.
  - *"How did you get to that kind of thinking?"*—This question is a little more direct than the previous one, as it states that the person doing the complaining is inextricably linked to the attitude they are taking on, and it forces them to do at least a little bit of self-reflection.
  - *"What do you need?"*—This question redirects toxic talk away from the students and refocuses it on the person speaking, helping them see what the real issue might be.
- **Tell a story:** Sometimes, the person complaining just needs to know that they are not alone. When they engage in toxic talk, tell them a story about a time you had similar feelings, but be sure to include in the story what you did about it and what the (hopefully) positive outcome you eventually reached was. Encourage them to try the solution that you included in the story so that it moves from complaint and inaction to something they can do to change the outcome for everyone.
- **Shut it down:** Sometimes, you just need to shut down the negative talk. A simple comment like "We don't talk like that here," "Let's keep it positive," or "Be nice"—delivered with poise and confidence from a veteran teacher like you—sends a clear message. Neuroscientists Andrew Newberg and Mark Robert Waldman (2012) back this strategy, explaining that "focus[ing] on negative words and thoughts . . . can actually damage key structures that regulate your memory, feelings, and emotions. You may disrupt your sleep, your appetite, and the way your brain regulates happiness, longevity, and health" (p. 24). These are very clear reasons to shut down toxic talk.

Saying Yes (and Saying No) to All Those Extras

When many of us were new teachers, we wanted to make a good impression. We also wanted to get hired back on our next contract. So when we were asked to serve on a committee, coach a team, or help out with an after-school activity, we may have replied with an emphatic "yes." And maybe we really enjoyed the opportunity. Or maybe it left us exhausted and imbalanced, trying endlessly to juggle what was in our regular job description (meeting with colleagues, planning lessons, and grading assignments, just to name a few) with the extra things we agreed to sign up for. Or maybe it turned into something we were, and continue to be, very passionate about.

These offers don't stop coming as new teachers become veteran teachers, but as teachers become experienced (and older), these extras can take an increased toll. As a veteran teacher deciding how and when to best invest your energy, first, take a deep breath. You don't need to say yes to everything anymore. (And hopefully, it hasn't taken you up to this point to realize this.) Maybe you've even gotten better and more comfortable saying no. But when it comes to all those committees and extracurricular activities, deciding what and how much to do can be a tricky process, no matter how many years you've been at it.

Figure 4.2 gives a quick look at what goes through many a person's mind when asked to participate in something extra.

"On the One Hand . . ."	"On the Other Hand . . ."
". . . they could really use someone with my experience!"	". . . I've done this already, and it's time for some new leadership."
". . . I'm really passionate about this!"	". . . I'm really passionate about a lot of things."
". . . they say they really need me for this to be successful."	". . . it might be successful, whether I'm involved or not."

FIGURE 4.2: Common thoughts when considering extras.

So how exactly do you decide whether to take on an extra? Try asking yourself the following questions.

- "Is it a capital Y-E-S with an exclamation mark? If not, can I say no and find something else to put my time into that's a *YES!*?"
- "What will be more uncomfortable: the temporary discomfort of saying no to this extra or the long-term discomfort of having to do this extra (until I have to face the discomfort of saying that I'm not going to do it anymore)?"

- "Is there an alternative I can offer, such as coleading with, suggesting, or mentoring a new lead?"
- "Am I so spent that all extras are a *no* right now?"

Acknowledge that if you say no to extras, it will be temporarily uncomfortable, but that feeling will pass! Then, write yourself a permission slip to follow your inner *YES!* to the activities that align with your goals for this stage of your career and life.

Having Difficult Conversations and Dealing With Conflict

As we stated at the beginning of this chapter, often the most sought-after leaders at a school are not the ones with the official titles or offices; rather, they are the ones that the other teachers quietly go to in their times of need. Sometimes, they go to this person for advice, and other times they ask for help in navigating a conflict with another colleague, a student, or a parent. And sometimes, the person they go to is *you*.

As a veteran teacher, you are well equipped to help. You've been around long enough that you have probably seen this situation before. You have the knowledge to advise and the wisdom to foresee what will happen if the conflict isn't dealt with. And yet, dealing with conflict can often be an icky, sticky thing that makes us very apprehensive and nervous. Even with a lifetime of experience, dealing with conflict is difficult!

Why is it so difficult? Because very strong emotions are involved, and that doesn't change with experience. (Sometimes, those feelings get even stronger as events in the present trigger emotions we might've thought long gone.) When someone is confronted with information that they perceive as threatening, demeaning, or challenging, the walls go up quickly. Mix this in with fear, rejection, and a lack of confidence in navigating these kinds of difficult conversations, and you can easily see why someone might want to avoid conflict.

It's also important to note that when conflicts are left unresolved, it can take an emotional toll on those involved. In their book *The Power of Teacher Teams*, Vivian Troen and Katherine C. Boles (2012) state:

> It's easy to avoid conflicts by never confronting serious issues and to achieve harmony by simply allowing only the more dominant members to have a voice in conversations. Yet successful teams do not shy away from conflict; rather, they understand that there are benefits to be gained from conflict resolution. (pp. 16–17)

As a veteran teacher, you've probably seen what happens when conflicts are left unaddressed, especially over long periods of time. Resentment and unhappiness build, ultimately leading to an inability to do our best work—the work that our students deserve from us.

There are generally two types of conflicts that arise at school: (1) the conflict that finds us and (2) the conflict that we must proactively address. Here's a look at both, as well as some guidelines on how to handle them.

Conflict That Finds You

You're in your classroom working on that lesson plan when a colleague enters your classroom with a problem. Maybe it's a problem with another colleague. They tell you their problem and expect an answer, but you're a bit thrown off by suddenly being confronted by this, and you're not sure what to do.

Not to worry. When someone drops a problem in your lap, your job is not to solve it but to hand it back to them (and to do so, as on *Jeopardy!*, in the form of a question). Asking people questions rather than offering advice actually makes them like you more (Huang, Yeomans, Brooks, Minson, & Gino, 2017). So take a deep breath and consider using one of the following.

- "Tell me more."
- "It seems like there might be more to this. What else?"
- "What do you need from me right now?"
- "What do you want the result of this conversation to be?"

All these questions get the person talking more and, hopefully, going a bit deeper into themselves regarding the issue at hand. (There is always an issue behind the issue. Consider the idea that all behavior is communication.) Equally important, asking a question will give you more time to process what is going on and to formulate a response. From there, you can decide how you want to proceed with handling the situation at hand. Sometimes, people just need to be heard. By responding to your questions and talking the issue through, they may find validation or resolution, with no further action needed.

Conflict That You Must Proactively Address

The type of conflict that is often more difficult to manage is the type that you need to handle proactively, either to stop something from happening or to minimize the "damage" once it's happened. Resolving such conflicts usually involves confronting a colleague about something they're doing, not doing, or needing to do differently. For many of us teachers, addressing a conflict with a student seems much easier, as it's "part of our job," whereas addressing a conflict with a colleague can make us feel very intimidated and ill equipped. This can be a bit trickier, and it definitely involves a process in order to know how to proceed. You don't need to be highly trained in the art of conflict management (but it would be nice!); you just need to be authentic, compassionate, and courageous.

When addressing a conflict, here are some steps you can take to help you navigate the conflict in a positive, effective way.

- **Before you have the conversation:** It's important to get into a clear, calm headspace *before* addressing a complex conflict. These tips can help you do that.
  - *Consider the conflict from multiple perspectives*—Before you approach your colleague, think about the issue from their perspective, your perspective, and perhaps your students' perspectives. This will help you enter the conversation knowing that there isn't only one perspective or only one answer.
  - *Make an appointment*—It never feels good to feel blindsided by a colleague. Timing matters when addressing conflict (Patterson, 2025). Reach out in advance of the conversation with a simple "Hey, I need to talk to you about something. When is a good time?" Or if you're already face to face, ask, "Is now a good time to talk?" That way, you have their permission to move forward with the conversation.
- **During the conversation:** When you're in the conversation, remain focused on the problem (not the person) and listen to understand (not to respond; Patterson, 2025). These tips can help you do that.
  - *Rehearse and open with confidence*—The first time you verbalize a conflict with a colleague should not be the first time you have thought about what you want to say. Think about it in advance and open the conversation with confidence. This will help you avoid *um*ing your way through the conversation instead of getting to the issue at hand.
  - *Be as specific as possible*—Try to avoid general statements. Be specific about what you want to address. For example, if you are addressing a colleague who regularly arrives late to your department meetings, instead of saying something general ("I really want to talk to you about how you are always late"), say something specific ("I noticed that you were ten minutes late to the meeting yesterday and fifteen minutes late the week before"). From there, the conversation should move toward listening to your colleague and making a plan to solve the issue.

- *Be real, listen, and find a way forward*—Confronting a colleague doesn't mean that you do all the talking. It might actually mean that you do most of the listening. Hear your colleague out and assure them that you want to find a path forward so that everyone can be happy and successful. With that said, work with them to make a plan. What needs to happen from here? Make a plan that everyone can stick to, and thank them for their time.

Addressing conflict can be quite a challenge, and being someone on your campus who makes that happen can be a tough gig. But your experience, know-how, and wisdom will improve your school, the profession, and the lives of students.

Final Thoughts

Be confident in who you are. You have dedicated many years and countless hours to our profession, and those around you have taken notice. You might not have been at your school the longest, but you've been around long enough that regardless of title or pay, you are a leader at your school.

You have built a skill set that others look toward when they need help, guidance, and encouragement. And those skills are apparent in all of the small and large ways that you lead each day—from the way you lead meetings, connect with parents and guardians, and navigate difficult conversations (often with parents and guardians) to the way you shut down toxic conversations with poise and confidence. Knowing clearly what you'll say yes and no to means you've got the critical skills every veteran teacher needs to finish strong.

CHAPTER 5

Sharing What You Know

As a veteran teacher, you've seen and experienced a lot during your career. Sharing what you know with other educators is a powerful way to empower others and foster collective growth. While it may seem commonplace for you, remember where you were at the start of your career. What is now obvious might not be to those less experienced.

Your career has provided you with many "You know . . ." moments, and we've shaped this chapter around what you know, with the hope that your colleagues (some new, some not so new) will reflect on what you have to share and will take the opportunity to grow in their own careers. We also hope that your reflections remind you to take pride in what you've done and to celebrate the difference you have made.

In this chapter, we cover how *you know* the following topics.

- (You know) who you are
- (You know) how education and your school work
- (You know) how there are hurdles along the way
- (You know) how to instill hope in students who feel hopeless
- (You know) how to navigate new schoolwide initiatives while having little time
- (You know) who you are is what you teach
- (You know) how you may not witness the fruits of your teaching

(You Know) Who You Are

You may have arrived at this profession eager to do everything you heard about, read about, or experienced as a student. Then, reality set in, and you might have felt that the demands of the role could exceed your capacity, but you coped! Eventually, you found your second (or maybe third or fourth) wind and hit your stride to become the valued teacher you are today. When talking about this experience, one colleague said the following to us:

> It is an unreasonable expectation that we get every aspect of our lives perfect every day. As I reflect on my time as a teacher, I know there were days when I was not the best teacher my students needed that particular day. What provides me solace is the notion that I tried not to let one bad day become a bad week. I tried to follow my struggles with a much better effort the next opportunity I had with that class. I choose to emphasize my responsibility, as that's all I really have control over.

You may have similar reflections, and the reality is that the nature of the work we do is a certain guarantee that not every day will generate a perfect score. But here's what reflecting on and acknowledging those moments reveals: Each time teachers choose to come back with a positive approach, the better the overall environment is.

Contrast this with an approach that holds on to the negative energy and experiences of the previous day and carries them forward on the following days. The result is an expanded negative environment where fear of reprisal dictates everyone's behavior. Every day has to represent a fresh start, which means letting go of all the negativity from the previous day or running the risk of the situation simply getting worse as you add new negativity to what you experienced the day before. How did you overcome those hard moments? What did you do to let them go and come back the next day prepared for a fresh start for yourself and your students?

Your Turn

How many years have you been a teacher, and how many colleagues have you had?

What are your strengths?

What are your growth opportunities?

What things have you learned or created during your career?

What about your career are you most proud of?

(You Know) How Education and Your School Work

One of the things you have as a veteran teacher is institutional memory (Potdar, 2023). While *institutional memory* usually refers to the collective knowledge, experience, and expertise accumulated within an organization over time, for teachers, there is an added layer: the institutional memory of what has happened over time at their school (assuming they've been there for several years), in their individual classrooms, and throughout the teaching profession. Policymakers enact laws and control budgets that deeply impact how our schools and districts operate and that directly influence what and how we teach.

As someone who has been around for a while, the memory you've built of all that has happened—internationally, nationally, and locally—is vital to the evolution of the teaching profession. Not only do trends come and go in our education world, but they often repeat themselves! While some veteran teachers might default to rolling their eyes and saying with a sigh, "Well, here we are again," you can use all that you know to help strengthen the work you and your colleagues do as well as the profession (Connelly, Černe, Dysvik, & Škerlavaj, 2019). Knowing can be half the battle, as you know. New teachers will not know what they *don't* know, and veterans often don't know what they *do* know. This phenomenon is called an *expert blind spot.*

Here are a few areas where your institutional memory can serve as a valuable resource.

- **Continuity:** The institutional memory you've built can help your school continue to evolve from year to year and from teacher to teacher. Sure, many schools have a well-crafted vision and mission statement (boldly displayed on the school's website), but often, the prevailing culture and attitude are passed down from the teachers who've been there to the new teachers who arrive. Your ability to articulate to your new colleagues what you've been doing, how things have changed or stayed the same, and what has worked and what hasn't is extremely valuable. With a team of veteran teachers, use the reproducible "Record of Efforts: What Worked, What Did Not" (page 68) to record this information, and then share it with colleagues to provide continuity of service and inform future decisions.
- **Decision making:** Few things are more frustrating to educators than when their school or district makes decisions that they feel are not in the best interest of students, teachers, or the community. Sometimes, a new principal or district administrator who hasn't been around for long makes those decisions. Your institutional memory holds information on everything from historical data, to initiatives that have and haven't worked (along with *why* they have or haven't worked), to lessons learned. In short, what you know can help less experienced colleagues make better choices and avoid repeat mistakes.
- **Knowledge and improvement:** Every successful industry continuously tries to improve. For industries that build products, improvement is usually measured in quality and profit. For educators, it's a lot more subjective. News of whether test scores are up or down from the previous year often serves as a model for the progress (or lack of progress) that we're making. And yet, we all know there's so much more to it. Your institutional memory can help serve as a foundation for capturing and sharing knowledge, and it can encourage your colleagues to build on and contribute to what you've learned, all in the name of continuous improvement. Here is one example: "Sharing of tacit knowledge among school staff helps create better environments for migrant students to integrate and feel like they belong at school" (NordForsk, 2025). Knowing why certain time periods (collaborative teacher time, for example) are considered nonnegotiable will help your colleagues understand the foundation success is built on.

Here's the bottom line: Your institutional memory is well earned, valuable, and critical to the success of your school and our profession. Don't be shy about sharing it!

Your Turn

Think about the institutional memory you have built over your years. Now answer the following.

The school that I'm at has a rich tradition in:

One of the things we're doing that has worked really well is:

One of the challenges that we're still struggling with is:

Well-earned information I have shared with some newer teachers includes:

Ways I will pass on more of my institutional knowledge before I go are:

(You Know) How There Are Hurdles Along the Way

In an opinion post for *Education Week*, education author Larry Ferlazzo (2025) identifies key areas that may explain why some choose an early departure from the teaching profession. As veteran teachers, you've most likely seen these and have found some ways to mitigate the impact while maintaining your positive contributions as a teacher.

- Students who are apathetic

- Students who are too far behind
- Students who are always on their phones
- Students who use generative AI to write their assignments

Let's look at each of these individually, along with a fifth challenge (students who are out of control in the classroom), and recall some of the strategies you employed to deal with each issue. Jot down some notes that you may want to share with colleagues the next time one of these topics comes up at a meeting.

Students Who Are Apathetic

Throughout your career, it's likely you've heard students resist a lesson, asking some form of "When am I going to use this stuff?" Relevance and reference points to their current lives shape students' interest in the material you want them to learn (and likely always have).

We're not suggesting that the solution lies in the need to become a social media sensation or an edutainer. Instead, we recommend tapping into students' interests. Ferlazzo (2025) suggests that "everyone is interested in *something*; it might just not be what *you* want them to be interested in." You can see how that overlaps with what psychologists Richard M. Ryan and Edward L. Deci (2000) identify as integral pieces of helping develop intrinsic motivation: relevance (personal value), autonomy (decision-making control), competence (capability), and relatedness (connection to others). Have your team of veteran teachers use the reproducible "Applied Self-Determination Theory" (page 69) to record ways each of you has incorporated these elements into your work, and share their responses with other staff members so they benefit from this institutional knowledge.

You know this is not about departing from foundational instruction; it's about including all four elements into your lessons and adding a little of your unique spice to your daily practice. Modeling this for your newer colleagues in particular may provide some insights for them as they adjust to the sometimes-overwhelming volume of content, as well as confront the misguided notions that everything in the curriculum guide must be touched and that every educator must do it the same way.

Your Turn

What thoughts did you have, as you read this section, about keeping students engaged?

Which of those thoughts will you share with colleagues?

Students Who Are Too Far Behind

Students don't all learn at the same pace, with some inevitably falling behind. In the early grades, that gap is relatively narrow, but if it's not addressed, it becomes more and more of an issue as students move to higher grades. Part of the challenge resides in the very organization of schools.

By and large, the only significant piece of evidence used in schools to sort students is their age. Almost all fourteen-year-olds enter ninth grade as freshmen in high school, with the assumption being that they are all at the same stage intellectually, socially, emotionally, physically, and academically. We know this is not accurate. Can you think of anything you've gotten better at over your career that you didn't demonstrate in the early stages? Weren't the majority of us "too far behind" as starting teachers? In fact, most readers of this book will identify things they got better at as adults that they rarely demonstrated as students in their own time.

Teachers can accelerate learning when they "identify and reinforce only the key concepts and skills that are absolutely necessary for students to understand in order to learn the more advanced lessons [they] are going to teach" (Ferlazzo, 2025). Think about the success you've had over your career in closing some of the gaps students arrived with. Did you focus on teaching less information better? Consider the fact that research on accelerated learning runs counter to practice in many schools:

> Sufficient evidence exists to encourage schools to take on the challenge of implementing effective differentiated pedagogy within heterogeneous classrooms. Ideally, such pedagogy would avoid the well-established negative effects of separate-class ability grouping while preserving opportunities for all students to access stimulating and challenging learning opportunities that are both suited to their present readiness level and geared toward pushing them to advance to higher levels of academic capability. (Nurenberg & Tuller, 2023, p. 3)

Shifting away from a strict structure of ability grouping and limited access to advanced courses means students in grade-level classes have more access to advanced coursework. It also means increasing the number of students—especially those who are from marginalized groups—in advanced courses. The research reveals that these shifts boost the academic achievement of *all* students in advanced courses (Nurenberg & Tuller, 2023).

Your Turn

What thoughts did you have, as you read this section, about some students having fallen too far behind?

Which of those thoughts will you share with colleagues?

Students Who Are Always on Their Phones

One of the expectations during the pandemic, driven by the reality of virtual learning, was that students would become more proficient on their devices. We have certainly seen the success of this! We've also seen the resulting challenge devices present in schools. Let's be clear: The devices students possess have unprecedented capability to divert students' attention to anything and everything happening in the world outside of your classroom.

Some of us have also been in this profession long enough to have seen other technologies, like the calculator, introduced. While the power of devices exceeds anything we've seen (with more challenges ahead), the response is likely one you've practiced and can share with some of your newer colleagues—especially about the responsible use of devices and a consistent schoolwide approach to managing their use. Ferlazzo (2025) points out the following about his experience: "Once *all* our teachers agreed to enforce a ban on cellphone use in class except when authorized by the classroom teacher, the problem became far more manageable at our school."

With over half of U.S. states and nearly all Canadian provinces and territories having some type of cellphone ban, there is support for the actions educators can take (Kircher & Holtermann, 2026; Quintet, 2025). More importantly, limiting such technology in the classroom can lead to academic improvement, with research showing "average test scores on the higher-stakes spring test [going] up by 1.1 percentiles more in the schools where students previously used their phones a lot, compared with low-activity schools" (Meltzer, 2025).

Again, while the device may be new, your experience in managing situations like this is a valuable tool to be shared. How you go about sharing it could be beneficial to colleagues who may just be looking at the most seemingly disruptive technology without having a historical perspective. (We get to generative AI next.) This speaks to how educators have responded over time to new challenges, and it emphasizes and strengthens the importance of a collective commitment to whatever approach you take as a school team. Share what you've learned over time when "we" agree on an approach but only "I" follow through on it.

Your Turn

What thoughts did you have, as you read this section, about student device use?

Which of those thoughts will you share with colleagues?

Students Who Use Generative AI to Write Their Assignments

As an extension of students' access to the internet via their devices, a challenge that has emerged is the incursion of generative AI. Teacher polls reveal a lack of—and need for—deep professional development on AI. If they receive any training at all, most of it reportedly "lack[s] critical elements that promote responsible student use of generative AI in ways that protect student privacy, safety, and civil rights," which impacts newcomers and veterans, since "this is leaving teachers to navigate practical management of generative AI use in the classroom on their own" (Dwyer & Laird, 2024, p. 12).

Educators also worry that students are using generative AI tools, like ChatGPT or Claude, for their work. That worry is real. The solution of using AI to detect AI is flawed, though common: "Teachers are becoming reliant on AI content detection tools, which is problematic given that research shows these tools are not consistently effective at differentiating between AI-generated and human-written text" (Dwyer & Laird, 2024, p. 13).

It's also important to remember that this will not be the first time students have used sources to get their work done. As a career educator, you've likely encountered tools ranging from graphing calculators to Wikipedia that impacted and changed how students approached their coursework. Whether it's Gemini for routine information searches, Grammarly for so-called enhanced writing, or Quizlet for automated grading and personalized study, what's important is "helping students learn about AI, its ethics, its shortcomings, and, yes, what it's good at, along with the advantages of not using it" (Ferlazzo, 2025).

Focusing on the process, not the product exclusively, is key. Think about the end product being an expository essay. If a teacher waits to intervene and assesses only when the essay is turned in, AI might be a lot easier to incorporate than if the teacher has been involved in every step of the process—from writing the introductory sentences, to constructing paragraphs, to revising various drafts.

Your Turn

What thoughts did you have, as you read this section, about student and teacher generative AI use, and which of those will you share with colleagues?

How is generative AI different from other tools you've integrated into school, and how does its impact move beyond the classroom?

What would you share with students and administrators (since not only new teachers should benefit from your institutional knowledge)?

Students Who Are Out of Control in the Classroom

If your impression is that student behavior has significantly changed since the 2020 pandemic began, your thoughts correspond with the majority of educators: In a 2023 survey, "more than 70% of teachers report[ed] a recent increase in disruptive behavior in the classroom compared to 66% in 2019" (Prothero, 2023, as cited in Whalen, 2025).

Luckily, classroom management is one of those skills most teachers get better at the longer they stay in the profession. While there may be some theoretical discussion of this concept during the time of a budding teacher's education program, it's never quite the same as that first day when they are leading their own classroom. Think back to that first day and reflect on the skills you've developed in this critical area. You figured out that the key to managing your classroom had less to do with repeatedly explaining how you wanted students to do something and more to do with clearly and intentionally explaining what you wanted done. You gave your students an opportunity to practice, reinforced the expectation, and then made sure it continued to be done—knowing that adjustments might need to be made along the way.

As we discussed, knowing who you are and what your strengths are will also play out in how you manage your classroom. Ferlazzo (2025) writes, "Positive relationships with students . . . are key: being friendly, not being friends." You've likely had former students come back and share that they appreciated you. It's more often than not related to the way you made them feel, rather than any brilliant lesson you delivered. That's gold to share with your newer colleagues before your time as an elite educator concludes.

Your Turn

What thoughts did you have, as you read this section, about classroom management?

Which of those thoughts will you share with colleagues?

What thoughts about an especially challenging student occurred to you as you read this section that you would want to share with colleagues?

(You Know) How to Instill Hope in Students Who Feel Hopeless

Teachers are merchants of hope for many. Every student who espouses hope does more than perform well academically. According to educator Michael Fullan (1997), "Hope is not a naive, sunny view of life. It is the capacity not to panic in tight situations, to find ways and resources to address difficult problems" (p. 221). Mathematician and educator Seymour Papert (1998) asserts that most skills students learn in school will be "obsolete" during their adulthood save one: "being able to learn." Consider how your teaching has instilled hope, which is linked to the ability to learn. If there is no hope, there is no need to learn. Papert (1998) explains that educators might do well to focus on teaching students "how to act when they're faced with situations for which they were not specifically prepared." In other words, fostering this hope in every student can help them face the challenges they will inevitably run into but have not been taught specifically to handle (Hierck, 2012b). Cultural and technological evolution demands it.

We educators can impact a student's level of hope by being mindful about what messages we send to them. "You didn't turn in this assignment," "You failed the quiz," and "You should participate more often" are messages that can make students feel like there is no break in their losing streaks, and that is dangerous:

> Disappointment leads to Discouragement. Discouragement leads to Disengagement. And, sadly, Disengagement is a short step away from Disappearance. These students leave our system with minimal skills and even less hope. In these situations poor choices are often the only choice. (Hierck, 2012b)

Your Turn

As you reflect on being a merchant of hope, how have you managed to instill this in your students?

What shortcuts or hacks have you learned? (A hack doesn't mean you avoid something; rather, it means you've learned to streamline it.)

What advice might you convey about how to build positive relationships with and instill hope in students?

(You Know) How to Navigate New Schoolwide Initiatives While Having Little Time

Think about the number of new ideas you have seen introduced during your career. How many of those were actually effective and made a difference for students and teachers? We're not here to suggest that education remains untouched by any other influences or that we should teach the same way that we always have. Teachers are abundantly aware of the changes in the world and ways to incorporate those changes. And we're certainly not suggesting that none of the initiatives introduced over time have had any merit. But if you reflect and share, you can help your newer colleagues.

We're not asking you to promote rebellion against the next thing that gets introduced but instead to help your colleagues and your leaders embrace the best aspects of change and maximize the value of that change. We're sincere about avoiding what educators at Creative Leadership Solutions (n.d.) talk about when they suggest:

> An exciting vision that is not implemented effectively does not inspire [teachers]; instead, it breeds cynicism among people who have seen one vision after another introduced with great fanfare only to quickly fade away, eclipsed by the next grand vision.

Think about what made the difference for you, what your role was in bringing the initiative to its best success, and how you carried influence with others on your team.

Your Turn

What initiatives introduced during your career felt important to support, and how did you sway your colleagues to support them?

How did you know when an initiative might be worth adding to your toolbox or when it made a positive difference?

What advice would you give current colleagues when the next new initiative gets floated?

(You Know) Who You Are Is What You Teach

Veteran teachers know that students see their every move. Even when we are not explicitly teaching content, our modeling is teaching students about expectations. Research shows that modeling can take several forms:

> Teachers express morality [what they consider "good behavior"] by their facial expressions, gestures and bodily postures, and they also spontaneously interject brief moral commentary on what is going [on] in the classroom, e.g., by giving a compliment or asking for students' attention. (Sanderse, 2024, p. 2)

What does your behavior convey to students, and does what you're saying without words ultimately mean "Do as I say, not as I do"? Don't make yourself the exception to classroom rules and norms. For example, do you not allow students to have food or drink in class, but then you show up with a mug of coffee? Modeling the behaviors you want students to emulate directly and positively impacts student behaviors (Blazar & Kraft, 2017). What message do you convey if rules apply to some and not everyone (Hierck, 2012a)?

And perhaps more importantly, students need specific guidance about what you are modeling in order to make an impression. Modeling without explanation may make no impact or may simply lead to imitation, so consider the need to encourage metacognition about student behaviors and "how [it] may help them to deal with future challenges," and share stories about your own behavioral choices and "how they both helped and hindered [you] to chart [your] own path in life" (Sanderse, 2024, p. 5). Tom shares the following:

> One of the best examples I saw of [modeling] was with a teacher who brought her "Bag of Me" with her to class. In that large bag were personal items that related to various times in the teacher's life. Students could pick out an item and the teacher then shared the story of why that item was significant. This built a positive relationship and provided a method by which students could also share their stories. (Hierck, 2012a)

If you're modeling a behavior for performance only in an effort to control behaviors, students will sniff out your insincerity and won't respond (Hierck, 2012a).

Your Turn

What's your best lesson in terms of its design, delivery, and ability to facilitate students' connection to their learning?

(You Know) How You May Not Witness the Fruits of Your Teaching

As a teacher who has been around a while, you've likely realized how short a typical school year is. With holidays and other assorted breaks, testing times, and family plans, there were years that just disappeared before you may have felt you had a chance to impact the students. This becomes even more difficult for those students who arrive with some challenges based on circumstances beyond our control. We have no control over the lives of our students once they leave school each day. We have little capacity to exert influence in the houses they live in and with the people who are raising them. Their personal lives that exist outside of school deeply influence their needs when they come to school. As the world becomes a smaller place, we have welcomed students who are from war-torn countries, who have spent time in refugee camps, and who don't speak the predominant language. None of this has derailed us from the work we do and the mission we are on. Although time with students may be limited, you've come to realize that every moment counts.

Throughout history, there has been no shortage of proverbs about teaching that speak to the passage of time. A saying commonly attributed to the Greeks professes, "Society grows great when old men plant trees whose shade they know they shall never sit in" (Goodreads, n.d.), and a proverb commonly attributed to the Chinese says, "The best time to plant a tree was 20 years ago. The second best time is now" (EXTRAordinary, n.d.). Regardless of the origin of these sayings, their underlying message is that sometimes, we might never see the impact of our work. While you may not see the immediate effects of your good work or ever enjoy the shade of the trees you plant, you are comfortable in the knowledge that you did all you could to ensure strong and steady growth so the end product was a great adult in a community somewhere.

Your Turn

What advice would you give your starting teacher self?

What three gifts—the precious things you've learned or developed over your career—would you give your new colleagues?

How have you maintained your motivation to teach? What do you owe your endurance to?

Final Thoughts

One of the most rewarding aspects of teaching is sharing your knowledge with others. Most often, we share our knowledge with students; however, sharing with colleagues, both in our schools as well as within the education profession, can be deeply gratifying (and sometimes, there are financial rewards as well!). This chapter focused on helping veteran teachers identify what, where, and how they can contribute what they've learned over their many years in the profession so education continues to evolve.

Sharing our passions, our struggles, and our true identities not only helps us personally but makes us all better teachers. It assists in building strong relationships, which are essential to creating both a positive classroom and a thriving school community.

You also recognize all of the hard work you have done and the great results you have achieved. Often times, teachers overlook these things as they approach the final years of their careers. Doing so serves to make any new challenges seem almost insurmountable. Having clarity on what you did to achieve greatness and adding your veteran insight to spot the challenges are invaluable assets to you and to the team you work with.

Record of Efforts: What Worked, What Did Not

With a team of veteran teachers, recall and record efforts that have occurred in your school. Respond to the following prompts and provide the information to administration and staff to increase continuity of service and inform future decisions.

What we have been doing (along with context about why and how):

How things have changed or stayed the same:

What has worked and why:

What has not worked and why:

Applied Self-Determination Theory

Psychologists Richard M. Ryan and Edward L. Deci's (2000) self-determination theory posits that four elements are integral to intrinsic motivation. As a team of veteran teachers, use this tool to individually record ways you have incorporated these elements into your work; then, share your team members' responses with other staff members so they benefit from your institutional knowledge.

Autonomy: Having some decision-making control over what needs to happen and how to do it

What strategies have you used to provide more voice and choice for students?

Competence: Feeling that we are capable of successfully doing what needs to be done

How have you helped students see and believe "I can succeed at this"?

Relatedness: Engaging in an activity that connects us to other people and feeling cared for by those we respect

How have you created opportunities that cross typical curricular or grade-level boundaries?

Relevance: Being shown content of interest that is valuable to us and useful for our present lives or future hopes

How do you connect the work today to what your students experience (or will experience as they continue their personal journey)?

Source for elements: Ryan, R. M., & Deci, E. L. (2000). Self-determination theory and the facilitation of intrinsic motivation, social development, and well-being. American Psychologist, 55*(1), 68–78.*

CHAPTER 6

Asking for Help (and Helping Others)

As teachers, we are drawn to helping others. For many, it's the reason for entering the profession. Also as teachers, we tell our students never to be afraid to ask for help. Yet it's something we often overlook when we're the ones who need help. Even as an experienced teacher, there are surely moments when you feel unsure of what to do or just plain stuck, stressed, or increasingly unhappy. While any veteran teacher can reflect on those times when they got unstuck and emerged stronger, it's important to recognize that you may also feel exhausted from years and years of getting yourself unstuck. Maybe you increasingly feel like you just don't have it in you to do the things that might've worked in the past.

This chapter outlines several situations and offers advice based on the real experiences of veteran teachers needing to ask for help. We also go deeper into how to express appreciation, both proactively and reactively, in an effort to build a truly collaborative culture where everyone thrives.

Here, we cover the following topics.

- Help for others
- Help for yourself

Help for Others

It can often feel more natural to help others than to get help for ourselves. Before you dig into the topic of helping yourself, we recommend thinking about your experience helping others—specifically colleagues. Applying the same approach to others as we do to ourselves can help us reframe our thinking about asking for and needing help. To that end, this section covers the following topics.

- Reflecting on a time when you helped someone else
- Understanding when to offer help

Reflecting on a Time When You Helped Someone Else

It's helpful to think about times in the past when you helped colleagues who themselves felt stuck. An essential skill in such support is the ability to control your own reactions, whether positive or negative. The ability to step back, analyze the situation, and then react in an appropriate manner is a key skill for working with colleagues and helping them move forward.

Reflections on the Journey: Looking Back to Move Ahead

I was in my fourth year of teaching, but really it was my first year for the fourth time. Each year I saw a completely different assignment (junior high science in my first year, alternative education and severe behavior in my second year, high school mathematics and science in my third year, and then a new community and school, as well as a return to a behavior program, in my fourth year), and little was related to my training to be a high school biology teacher. (Thus far, I had managed to teach one block of that.) I had no training in behavior or special education and little in mathematics. I was feeling very stuck.

Thankfully, a veteran took me under his wing and was my "foster teacher" for the first six months. From covering practical and seemingly mundane things like schedules and the school layout (I was teaching in multiple rooms, and knowing the shortcuts was a time saver!) to reviewing what he knew about some of my students and their assets, to inviting me to lunch with the team, he really helped me get settled and established. I'm not sure I would have remained a teacher, and yet, here I am, forty-one years later, still working in education.

—Tom Hierck

Guiding others is not always easy, and it's especially tempting to want to provide all the answers along with the advice. It can be very challenging to hold back on offering immediate problem-solving advice and allow colleagues to process, sharing only key insights (when asked for them) along the way.

This suspension of opinion is crucial to helping others as they work through challenges. With education author John Eller, Tom describes *temporary suspension of opinion* as:

> an internal skill that allows the receiver of communication (the listener) to withhold sharing an opinion about the message he or she heard from the sender. *Suspension* is used to increase the opportunity of thinking and problem solving on the part of the sender. (Eller & Hierck, 2021, p. 35)

It's tempting, and very easy, to want to move in to give advice too quickly. This can lead to finishing someone else's sentences, giving opinions, or not listening to what someone has shared because you are busy thinking about the solution you will present. There is also the danger of unintentionally making ourselves the focus when we are trying to connect (Chaiken & Bierly, 2025). When we do this, we risk colleagues tuning out before they hit their stride. Consider the following three levels that people experience while temporarily suspending their opinions during a conversation (threefold consulting, 2015).

1. **Listening level:** The focus is on the other person and requires you, the listener, to suppress your need to talk. Sometimes, by listening, we allow the other person to better hear and understand their own problem or issue.
2. **Diagnostic level:** You're listening, processing, and analyzing. You don't share until the speaker has finished, and only if they ask for input.
3. **Emotional level:** The response part is often the most challenging. It's tough not to get drawn in or appear to support some of the raw emotion that might come up while remaining clear headed.

Especially at the emotional level, you may find yourself relating to the speaker or feeling dysregulated emotionally. Before responding with something like "The same thing happened to me" or "That reminds me of when . . .," validate the other person's feelings (Chaiken & Bierly, 2025). That might sound like "That must have been really difficult" or "This makes sense to me." This skill often depends on the listener's mindset or attitude. The positive offshoot of practicing this skill is that it also builds a better relationship over time with the colleague you've assisted.

Figure 6.1 (page 74) illustrates these levels.

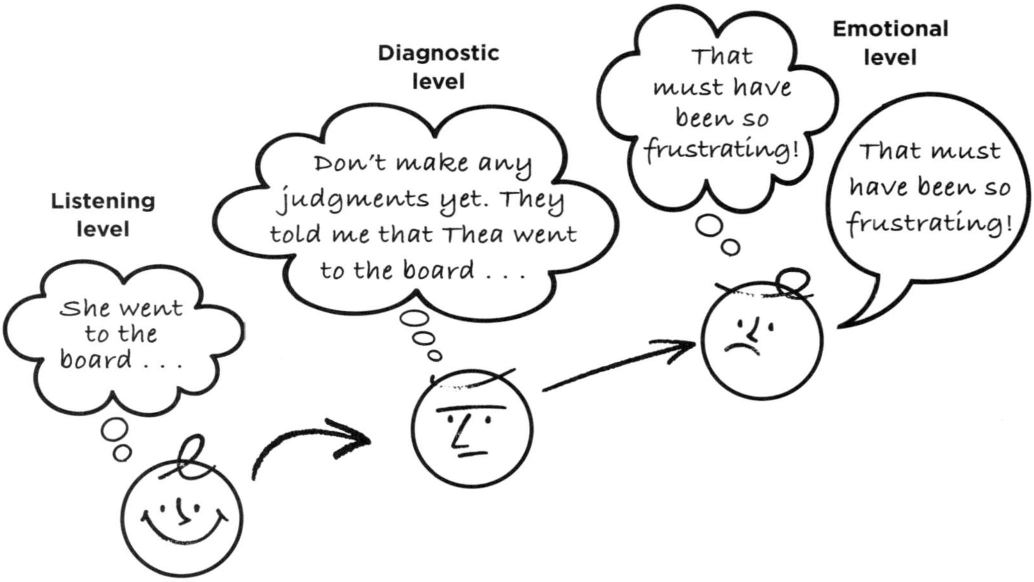

Source: Adapted from Eller & Hierck, 2021; threefold consulting, 2015.

FIGURE 6.1: Temporarily suspending an opinion.

Your Turn

How does the Reflections on the Journey narrative (page 72) resonate with you?

How many colleagues have you been able to reconnect with their passion and purpose when they got despondent over their career choice?

Think about a situation where you were able to help a colleague get unstuck. What was the situation? How did you help them process through (get unstuck)?

Understanding When to Offer Help

A strong, committed team overcomes challenges that a loose affiliation of individual talent will never surmount. Think of the individual talent that exists in every school and imagine that variety of talents rallying around a common focus with an unrelenting approach. When struggles occur, the members of the team turn to each other, look each other in the eye, and say, "We've got this." What a powerful group that is, and what an unstoppable force!

Now, think about what you, as the veteran teacher, bring to that team. You are a vital part of the team based on all you've seen and done. And while experience counts, so does a desire to keep learning, and that's where you might be at your most inspirational. Your experience and your observational and metacognitive skills allow you to consider when you need assistance. Add to that being proactive and direct, and your support will be appreciated. Remember, as a new teacher, you were overwhelmed and likely couldn't even formulate what you needed. As a veteran, it may be that you can offer specific assistance rather than a general comment like "I'm here if you need help." Saying "Let's meet today to go over report card procedures or Meet the Parents night" is likely to generate a better, more authentic response.

Help for Yourself

It's very likely that during your career, you've had moments when you have felt stuck—trapped, stagnant, or unsure how to move forward. Maybe it was that student who pushed all your buttons (and discovered a new one that you didn't know even existed). Or maybe it was older students who burst out in class despite having been told, for many years, that that was not desirable behavior. It's a frustrating and disheartening feeling that has the potential to be a lonely experience that leads to isolation. For some, this may represent a short-term pause before finding clarity and getting their teaching mojo back. Left unchecked, however, being stuck could last months, significantly impacting mental well-being, health, and overall satisfaction (Grant, 2013). Then, the role of teacher seems more of a chore than a choice.

Part of the challenge of being stuck is that the feelings snowball, and the pressure to do better and be better can feel overwhelming. Releasing this need for perfection is a prerequisite for progress. The fear of not measuring up can truly hinder or paralyze teachers and is one of the most common reasons teachers feel stuck. In *You're a Teacher Now! What's Next?*, we talk about the moments as a teacher "where you feel like you have absolutely no idea what you're doing . . . It's OK, and it's totally normal" (Hierck & Kajitani, 2024, p. 32). Even veteran teachers, who have been at it for many years, experience impostor syndrome, which can keep them mired in their world of doubt. To that end, the following sections cover these topics.

- Understanding what it means to get stuck and unstuck
- Identifying why you are stuck
- Recognizing when you need help

Understanding What It Means to Get Stuck and Unstuck

How can teachers move forward and get unstuck? Try shifting your focus from the fear of failure to the recognition that it's normal to experience bumps on the journey. (Remember the acronym FAIL, which stands for *first attempt in learning*.) Failure is not the end but instead a stepping stone on the journey toward growth. Every teacher's journey is unique, driven by their experiences, expertise, and passion. We've all had singularly unique lives up to this point and have some unique keys to unlock learning, both for our students and ourselves.

When you have moments where you can't seem to move through these feelings, try the following ideas.

- Meditating or deep breathing
- Engaging in movement or exercise (walking, stretching, doing yoga)
- Drinking water
- Repeating positive affirmations and adjusting your mindset
- Talking through your feelings with a trusted friend, a family member, or even a counselor

As far as combating the impostor syndrome that has you stuck, consider the following suggestions:

- **Think about a past accomplishment:** Maybe even reflect on a time that you felt unprepared for the task at hand. What did you do, and how did it turn out? Chances are you got through it and learned a lot. Whatever the outcome, it helped get you to where you are today.
- **Go next door:** Pop in to see a colleague you respect and let that person know how you're feeling. Ask how they deal with [*insert whatever you're feeling uneasy about*]. You'll probably find that you leave feeling a lot better than when you walked in.
- **Look into the future:** Think about how you're feeling now, and then think about how you want to feel a year, or several years, from now. The only way to get there is to go through it. Remember that every accomplished teacher has been where you've been, felt what you've felt, and gotten through it. You will, too!

- **Find a way to laugh:** When we laugh, we put things in perspective. Whether it's watching that video that always makes you smile or calling that friend who always makes you laugh, find something that redirects your angst and helps you remember that the job you do is also silly, funny, and wonderful. (Hierck & Kajitani, 2024, p. 32; brackets in the original)

Stepping out of your comfort zone by taking that initial step is a powerful way to make progress and move toward getting unstuck. In fact, it might be the only way. Once you've embraced imperfection and taken that first step, you'll gain momentum. Celebrate the small victories and build on them, adapting as you go.

It's also helpful to recognize that the nature of the work you do, the relationship-focused aspects of the work, and your total commitment and passion might mean that getting stuck could happen again. You will get better at recognizing the signs and getting unstuck. You've got this!

Your Turn

Think about a time in your career where you got stuck. What was the situation? How did you work through it to get unstuck?

How can your colleagues today benefit from that experience?

Identifying Why You Are Stuck

Knowing why you are feeling down or stagnant can sometimes be more difficult than you might expect. If we take an overall look at the challenges facing educators, that can be a starting point for identification. Education authors Peter M. DeWitt and Michael Nelson (2026) identify the following critical issues facing teachers.

- Social media
- Mental health
- Empowerment of parents and caregivers
- Artificial intelligence
- Literacy proficiency
- Mathematics proficiency
- Primary grade- or course-level instruction (also known as *Tier 1*)
- Teacher collaboration
- Principal attrition
- Teacher attrition

Any one of these can be overwhelming and has the potential to derail you from bringing your best self to work each day. The good news is that your experience will help you tackle most of this list. There is also the potential for you to learn from colleagues—especially some of the newer ones—on topics related to *their* skill set. As a general statement, most of our younger colleagues trend toward being pretty good with technology, and they might be the first people you check in with on topics like generative AI and social media. (They just have a better grasp than some of us veteran teachers!)

Beyond this list of current issues exists the potential to get stuck because of the routine nature of your role. Have you been in the same area or expertise for a number of years? Do you know not only next week's lesson but also next month's and next term's? As a famous lyric from a U2 (2000) song so poignantly states, "You've got stuck in a moment / And now, you can't get out of it."

The good news resides in two qualities we're pretty certain you already possess.

1. Your experience means you may have gone through this before and have a reference point as to how to get out of the rut.
2. Your skill set possesses such a variety of tools that even though this might be a novel rut, you have the talent to navigate over, under, around, or through it.

Recognizing When You Need Help

Not everyone who is stuck needs help, but remaining open to asking for help is important. One of the challenges in being a veteran teacher is the notion that you must always present yourself as competent, clear, and on top of everything. Too often, first-year teachers feel this pressure and rarely complain. A variety of factors influence this, including the desire to appear capable, the potential for negative feedback, and the pressure to adjust to a demanding new role. All of these factors are occurring while first-year teachers are attempting to build relationships with students and colleagues and learning to navigate the complexities of a school system. This reality is the reason why first-year teachers are 2.5 times more likely to quit the teaching profession than more experienced teachers (Fantilli & McDougall, 2009). Additionally, attrition rates for new teachers are remarkably high, "reaching up to 40 percent in the first five years in Canada, the UK, and the US" (Perry, 2025). While new teachers might feel more reluctant to ask for help from veteran teachers, veteran teachers still get stuck, too. They may also be reluctant and may feel *more* pressure to ride it out rather than ask for help.

Knowing What the Signs Are

Experience does not excuse veteran teachers from the need to seek help. It almost seems like once the newness of being a teacher has worn off, the pressure not to seek help comes from a feeling of "I ought to know how to do this." It's OK to be stuck and need time to process through that, as many readers of this book will attest to. There may even be moments you feel so overwhelmed that quitting feels like the best option. Reach out and ask for help if you find yourself feeling that way or focusing on the following challenges (Lodwick, 2023).

- The impossibility of doing all that is on your plate (with more to come)
- The task requirements you are most familiar with changing (such as moving from a 0–100 point grading scale to a 4 point rubric)
- Technological advancements exceeding your comfort level, leaving you to wonder whether younger colleagues would be better team members

Turning to informal supports (such as teacher colleagues), attending regular team meetings, and having a supportive and visible leader are all positive factors that help teachers grow in the profession.

Knowing Why Asking for Help Is Hard

One of the real challenges for teachers (and for people in general) is to ask for help. However, when we don't learn to ask for help, we limit our progress. We make things harder for ourselves when they could be easier. This reluctance to ask for help reinforces unhealthy expectations for us, sets up a standard that discourages vulnerability, and limits our potential. For some teachers, this reluctance may be deeply rooted and could be one of their earliest school memories. Perhaps they were shamed for asking for help or saw someone face consequences for showing that they didn't have the answer.

We also witness the praise heaped on those who seemingly have all the answers and are lauded as "self-made" practitioners. Psychoanalyst Manfred F. R. Kets de Vries (2023) identifies a variety of reasons, including the following, that asking for help can be such a challenge.

- **The fear of being vulnerable:** Asking for help can feel like a sign of weakness for people who worry about how others perceive them. They fear seeming incompetent or inferior. As we discussed previously, some might also have impostor syndrome. It's almost easier to be highly competent at the wrong stuff than to have to be (temporarily) ineffective and try to grow.

- **The need to be independent:** Asking for help can feel uncomfortable to someone who makes self-reliance and self-sufficiency priorities. As we mentioned, some of our earliest school experiences align with needing to demonstrate independence and not count on others. Familial and cultural backgrounds also play a role in these early beliefs, with individuals believing they *should* be able to do everything solo. These adults are challenged when there is emphasis on collaboration because their self-image hinges on independence.
- **The fear of losing control:** As teachers, there is an element of control to the work we do, with structure and routine being critical components to our success. Asking for help might put you in an uncomfortable spot where you are beholden to someone. Some people might find it a challenge to overcome trust issues and might want to avoid putting themselves at risk by relying on others. The power shift that comes with asking for help could make them uneasy. Consequently, some people are more comfortable carrying problems individually.
- **The fear of rejection:** Asking for help puts one at risk of rejection (if someone can't or refuses to help), and some people believe rejection is an attack on their self-worth. When combined with some of the other reasons in this list, that rejection can be devastating. If your appeal is refused, think about the courage it takes to be vulnerable and the repercussions associated with that (such as wondering whether confidentiality will be kept, whether the person now thinks differently of you, or whether you'll have the courage to bring another issue forward). In that moment, it can be hard to imagine that the reason someone said no to helping has nothing to do with you but everything to do with something totally unrelated to you.
- **The tendency to overempathize with others:** As teachers, we generally fall pretty high on the empathy scale. Some people are so attuned to other people's emotions that they anticipate reactions ("I know just how you feel") that might not materialize. They avoid asking for help to keep from burdening others or being seen as a nuisance or as selfish. Instead, they continue taking care of and protecting others while hiding or ignoring their own needs.
- **A sense of victimhood:** Asking for help can be painful for people who believe they don't deserve it. A persistent inner voice may lead them to believe they must struggle alone. They compare their situations to others' and resolve that it's their lot in life and that they deserve all that happens. For those in this situation, seeking help doesn't occur because the problem seems justified.

This list may serve as an opportunity for reflection during challenging moments or as a reminder of your response to those challenges. There may come a time when your energy flags, and you need motivation and a reminder that you have done difficult things and can continue doing them.

Being a veteran doesn't mean you'll never have to ask for help. Asking for help may always be a challenge. It requires being vulnerable and may butt up against intentional or unintentional lifelong lessons. As a veteran teacher, you've experienced so much, and it's that experience that will help you. Being a veteran teacher *does* mean being clear, concise, and specific when asking for what you need, as well as expressing gratitude for the support. Asking for help could be as simple as requesting a quick favor with a task or as significant as seeking advice on something that requires greater support ("I'm struggling with [issue] and could use some guidance"). It's inspiring for everyone when a veteran still models growth, driven by a desire to address an area of struggle.

Final Thoughts

When feeling stuck as a teacher, it's helpful to take a step back and address both your physical and mental well-being. This can involve practices like meditation, exercise, and time in nature. Even as a veteran teacher, you might consider reaching out to colleagues or mentors for support and inspiration. Reflecting on your career, remembering the mission you are on (and the difference you are making), and taking small, sometimes-imperfect actions can help you gain momentum and move forward.

CHAPTER 7

Planning for Retirement

For some, the word *retirement* brings forth daydreams of hammocks on beaches, time in the garden, or playtime with grandkids. For others, the word brings about a massive sense of uncertainty, as well as a fear of boredom, a loss of self, and financial insecurity. And, of course, others are somewhere in between. Regardless of where you're at, accept it, embrace it, and move forward to set yourself up for success. You have your days, your finances, and your health to attend to.

It's never too early to begin retirement planning emotionally and practically—something many of us apparently avoid. Consider a report that reveals that "fewer than 30 per cent of Canadians have emotionally prepared for retirement, making the transition more difficult than many expect" (Mohammed, 2025). Researchers at John Hancock and the MIT AgeLab (2025) tell us that one of our biggest planning gaps is for continuing care, which 70 percent of older adults in the United States will require eventually. Their eye-opening Longevity Preparedness Index indicates that people score a 42 out of 100 on preparedness for continuing care—which we know is a failing grade.

In this chapter, we address some of the most critical considerations as you begin to look toward official retirement, and we even go a bit past retirement. And, of course, everyone is different, so regardless of where you are in your timeline when you start looking at this chapter, remember that our suggestions are only guidelines. You determine your path.

While getting retirement "right" is a goal for some people who have retirement in their sights, keep in mind that this book's subtitle focuses on "staying happy, healthy, and highly effective" in the years leading up to it.

With that, this chapter helps you explore the following topics.

- Preparing for retirement's phases
- Knowing your years-of-service numbers
- Budgeting for your future
- Prioritizing your (physical and mental) health
- Pursuing a project, passion, or activity (starting now)
- Understanding upcoming identity changes
- Thinking about where you want to live
- Planning your retirement party

Preparing for Retirement's Phases

Something that is important to remember is that retirement isn't a singular event. In fact, "psychologists stress that retirement is a process" (Mohammed, 2025). Just like your teaching career has moved through phases, your retirement will as well. Seminal research from gerontologist Robert C. Atchley (1976) indicates six phases (as cited in LaRue, 2022).

1. **Preretirement:** At this point, expectations about what retirement will be are forming.
2. **Retirement:** This is also known as the honeymoon phase, where retirees enjoy their new free time. This phase usually occurs between six months to two years after retirement begins. Mentally, this is a positive time.
3. **Disenchantment:** Here is where retirees may be prone to developing depression, with the "Canadian Psychological Association report[ing] that up to 25 per cent of new retirees experience symptoms of anxiety or depression in their first year—often due to a loss of structure, identity, or community" (Mohammed, 2025).
4. **Reorientation:** At this stage, retirees shift, adjusting their interests and self-perceptions, leading to a more realistic understanding of what retirement holds.
5. **Retirement routine:** Day-to-day life is more stable at this point. Retirees have settled in.
6. **Termination of retirement:** Health and age-related issues disrupt the previously established routine.

Being aware of these stages can help you set expectations. The more realistic your expectations, the more likely you are to feel good about where you are. Former teacher Ron Jeffery (2023) recommends creating two lists.

1. Goals you have set and achieved
2. Ways you can achieve the still-unmet goals and the resources you need to do so

To generate these lists, consider the following questions: "What was [my] bucket list? Are there things [I] can still achieve either with help or individually? Do [I] have a purpose each day for what [I] can achieve?" (Jeffery, 2023). Having a firm sense of self can make a difference in your contentment and mental health as you plan for and experience retirement. Career and retirement counselor Brian Lambier advises:

> A lot of people define who they are by what they do. . . . So [they ask] how do I replace that? . . . You need something a lot deeper, that resonates more with who you are as a person, what your value system is, what you're passionate about, who the people you want to hang out with are. You need to really understand yourself at a deeper level. (as cited in Mohammed, 2025)

Getting a handle on your years-of-service numbers is one way to manage those expectations.

Knowing Your Years-of-Service Numbers

Every state or province—and sometimes school district—has different retirement formulas for when the optimal time to retire is. Of course, *optimal* is subjective, going beyond numbers and money. Only *you* can decide when the time is right for it, but understanding what benefits you will receive when you retire is a critical variable in the equation.

Research indicates that many teachers are planning their retirement finances but have some gaps in their learning. RAND's American Teacher Panel reports:

> While most teachers are taking steps to prepare for retirement, many teachers do not currently possess the basic retirement knowledge necessary to plan effectively. Teachers struggled to identify their plan type, how much they contribute to their plans, retirement eligibility ages, and who contributes to Social Security. (Fuchsman, McGee, & Zamarro, 2024, p. 1)

In some U.S. states, the difference in benefits you'll receive when retiring at sixty-two versus sixty-seven versus seventy is substantial. Whatever the benefits look like for you, you'll need to weigh those numbers in consideration of when you *want* to retire. For some, hanging in there another five years is totally worth the extra payout; for others, the payout is less important. In Canada, look at your province's pension plan to make your personal calculations. Your provincial teachers' association should provide resources for this. Also, note that every province has a retired teachers' association that provides helpful budgeting resources when you reach retirement, as does the Association Canadienne des Enseignantes et des Enseignants Retraités or, in English, the Canadian Association of Retired Teachers (ACER-CART). (Visit https://acer-cart.org for more about its resources.)

Regardless, having a good financial adviser and meeting with your district's benefits person (they should *not* be the same person) are important steps toward understanding those numbers. Do not wait to do this. Knowing these numbers *before* you're ready to retire (as far before you're ready as possible) gives you time to (a) know what you're working toward, (b) start or continue saving additional money to supplement what you'll be receiving in retirement, and (c) make any adjustments along the way. When you meet with your benefits person, you will probably have a lot of questions. The questions in the reproducible "Benefits Contact Questions" (page 95) should be on your list.

It's also important to note that things change. Policy changes, the economy changes, and your personal situation changes, so tracking these things ten or more years out gives you an opportunity to adjust and rethink and hopefully continue to invest in your future.

Budgeting for Your Future

Some of us are really good at creating and sticking to a budget. Others of us, well—it hasn't exactly been something we've been living by, especially when our expenses have been all over the place with the needs of day-to-day life. However, retirement forces many of us to live within a strict budget. For some, this can be very difficult, as their earning potential goes down, and the money they get from pensions, savings accounts, and so on isn't as much as when they were working full-time. For others, the predictability of the money coming in actually makes it easier to budget, plan, and say no to things. (You can always have a ready answer like "Sorry, I'm retired now and living on a fixed budget, so I can't go on that trip that I don't really want to go on anyway!")

When it comes to managing money and budgeting for retirement, here are a few tips that might work for you.

- **Remember that time is your friend:** It may seem obvious, but the more time your savings grow in retirement accounts and other investments, the better. That also means you'll have more time to recover when markets are in decline. For example, Alex and his wife bought their first home before a stock market crash, but by holding on to it, they gained equity and earned money from its sale. There are plenty of books, people, and programs out there that will tell you where and how to invest your money. This book isn't one of them, but we do advise seeing a financial adviser you like and trust to put together a plan for how much to save for retirement. Prior to that appointment, you might read *Where to Spend, Where to Save: A Teacher's Guide to Managing Your Finances* (Kofke, 2026), which has educator-specific retirement savings information.

- **Remember that budgeting for retirement can be tough:** You don't know what your exact expenses will be, what might happen in your life, and (of course) how long you'll live. (If you do, we'd love to put that in our next book!) However, it's a good idea to start focusing on what kind of budget you'll have when you retire. If you're still several years out, consider trying out a practice period where you try sticking to the budget that you anticipate needing in retirement. That practice can help you see how much money you will need and spend and whether you can live within your means. It's far better to know and be able to make adjustments well in advance than to realize after you have retired that you budgeted poorly. That said, make sure you factor long-term care into your planning budget, an expense many people forget.
- **Consider that expenses often change (and rarely go down):** Keep in mind that adult children often still need financial support, medical expenses rarely decrease, and the need for someone to drive you places is costly. Work with a financial expert who will know how to include the unknowns in your plans. After all, "it's important to be prepared for the hidden costs of retirement. Those unexpected expenses often derail people's retirement plans, such as a healthcare emergency or long-term care expenses" (City National Bank, n.d.). If your planner doesn't bring them up, ask about unexpected types of expenses, such as major home repairs and upgrades and unanticipated travel to help relatives. If your budget for hiring a financial planner is tight or nonexistent, check out organizations such as the National Association of Personal Financial Advisors (NAPFA) or the Canadian Foundation for Financial Planning (CFFP), which offer reduced-fee and pro bono financial planning services.
- **Check in with your trusted friends, family members, and former colleagues who have retired:** One of the best things you can do to prepare for retirement is to learn from the successes and mishaps of those who have faced retirement before you—especially if they worked in the same district as you, live in the same general area, and live similarly to what you envision your life will look like financially after you retire. What did they plan well for? What did they not anticipate? What would they have done differently? What advice would they give to someone who is planning to retire in ________ years? Asking questions like these can help set you up for success when it's your turn!

The reproducible "Financial Experts" (page 97) can help you keep track of your contacts for important planning (or even help you begin seeking references to potential professionals you want to hire).

Prioritizing Your (Physical and Mental) Health

As teachers, we've spent a *lot* of time caring for others' well-being. As a result, many of us have put off our own needs. You may believe you will start to take better care of yourself once you have more time. Caring for yourself is not selfish. Prioritizing your health well *before* you retire will not only help you be a happier, healthier teacher now (which benefits both you and your students), but it could also lead to you beginning retirement feeling how you want to feel, rather than starting that process once you retire. According to a study on retirees' happiness, nearly half of those who reported being happy in retirement said that they prioritized their health when planning for retirement (Business Wire, 2024; MassMutual & PBS Insights, 2024).

In addition, taking advantage of your healthcare benefits when you are working full-time might be much less costly than when you are retired and using different benefits. Proactively taking care of any health issues you have well *before* you retire can make you feel better in the immediate years to come, as well as potentially help you glide into retirement much stronger and more able to tackle whatever health issues arise later.

Once you retire, you might find yourself at an interesting crossroads: You have more time to be active and to devote to your health, but, well, you're getting older, and things may hurt a bit more than they did when you were younger. See figure 7.1 for a visualization of these considerations.

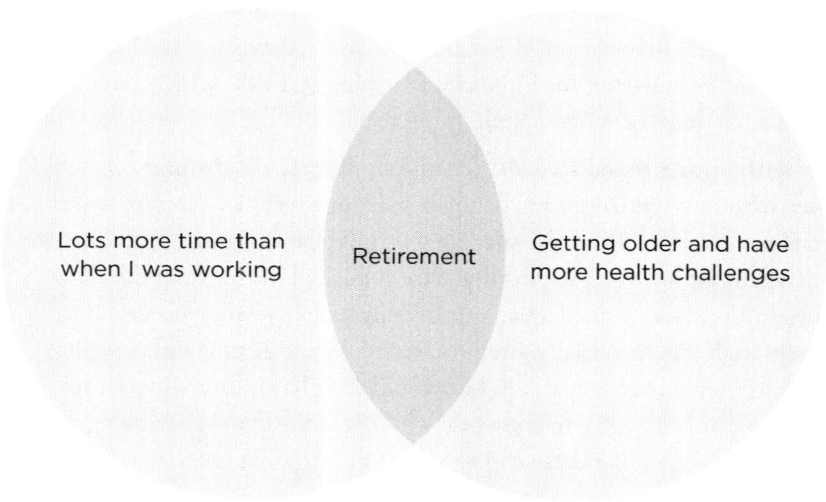

FIGURE 7.1: Venn diagram of health considerations.

Along with prioritizing your physical health, looking ahead at how you will stay happy and mentally healthy is critical as well. According to that same study, nearly one-third of retirees report feeling lonely sometimes, and those who report being happy often spend their free time exercising, pursuing hobbies (more on that in the next section), traveling, and being with loved ones (Business Wire, 2024; MassMutual & PBS Insights, 2024).

So what's the bottom line? Just as it's important to start saving money well before you retire, think about addressing your health issues and building your social circles well *before* you retire so that when you do, you can enter retirement with friends and a plan in place. Two areas we focus on next are pursuing a project, passion, or activity (starting now) and understanding upcoming identity changes. These two approaches do much to prioritize your physical and mental health.

Pursuing a Project, Passion, or Activity (Starting Now)

Have a hobby, activity, or passion that you really want to pursue once you retire? This stage of your life and career can be a perfect time to try that thing for the pure joy of it. It's also a time that some people want to really challenge themselves to master a new skill. In his book *Outliers: The Story of Success*, Malcolm Gladwell (2008) popularizes a concept known as the *10,000-hour rule*, which is often referred to as the *10-year rule*. It basically says that to achieve mastery at something, you need to devote about ten-thousand hours of focused practice to that pursuit. So if it's going to take ten years to get good at something, why not start now? When you retire, you'll already be good, so you can skip the required beginner period.

Of course, we're not guaranteeing that you'll reach expert level in this specified amount of time, but if you start pursuing whatever you want to pursue now, by the time you retire in ten years, chances are you'll already be pretty good at it, and retirement will give you time to get even better! It is also often the case that as we get more skilled at something, we begin to enjoy it more, so this might be an opportunity to begin retirement with more time to do what you love, instead of finding something that you love! There are concrete benefits to pursuing activities of interest, whether just for fun or for mastery. They can often put you in contact with other people with similar passions—and the size of your social network directly impacts your physical and mental health (Pilehvari et al., 2023).

Your Turn

What's something you would like to be better at doing five years from now? Ten years from now?

What could you do to get started on these now?

Understanding Upcoming Identity Changes

Being a teacher is a huge part of our identity. When we meet someone new and they ask, "What do you do?," the words "I'm a teacher" usually roll off our tongues with enthusiasm and ease. As teachers, we often associate our identity with our career. But when you are retired, you lose a portion of your identity. It's entirely normal to grieve that part of ourselves when we move into retirement (Atchley, 1976; Parkin & Winsborough, 2025), and the "space between work and retirement can be a profound challenge to one's self-concept. It is particularly difficult for people who have succeeded in knowledge-based professions where cognitive performance and expertise are fundamental to professional identity" (Parkin & Winsborough, 2025).

Just because you're retired doesn't mean you're no longer a teacher. For some new retirees, this reality hits hard—not when they first retire but when the new school year begins. They suddenly find themselves *not* setting up their classroom, attending back-to-school trainings, and having those dreams of being completely unprepared for the first day of school. At Atwater Elementary School District in Atwater, California, all retired teachers from the district are invited to attend the back-to-school kickoff rally on the teachers' first day back. They sit together, enjoy coffee and snacks, and interact with their colleagues who are still working full-time. Many report that attending this event not only removes the feeling that the school year is starting without them but provides a sense of relief, as they get a good reminder that they're still part of the school district, but they don't need to run to their classroom to get everything set up.

Also, remember that you're just switching one identity for another. Focusing on what you *are* can be very helpful in the transition to retirement. This often comes with the new roles you might be taking on. What makes you valuable beyond your in-classroom skills? What are you doing that is bringing you the most joy? Are you a grandparent? Mentor? Caregiver? Gardener? Activist? Whatever it is, take the time to grieve what you are no longer, and then embrace what you are now and what you are becoming.

Retiring from teaching is a wonderful time to invent (or reinvent) yourself. It's an opportunity to write yourself a new story. Try making an identity story where you look at the events, choices, and threads of your life and then create an empowering narrative for yourself about who you are and what your personal evolution was. Researchers find that those who made such stories were "better able to make peace with their transitions and leave behind their old identities, expressing more positive sentiment about their currents [*sic*] situations than those who did not craft such stories" (Toubiana, Ruebottom, & Hakak, 2022).

Keep in mind that retiring from teaching doesn't mean you are no longer teaching. Many teachers choose to continue working on a part-time basis or to volunteer. Whether it's helping support struggling readers at the local library, teaching a few classes in a college education program, or pursuing one of the endless possibilities (both inside and outside of teaching) that you'll now have time for, embracing who you are and who you are evolving to be will go a long way in you staying happy and feeling good about how you are spending your time. As Bonnie Prudden states, "You can't turn back the clock. But you can wind it up again" (as cited in Schroeder, 2024).

Thinking About Where You Want to Live

A multitude of decisions factor into where you want to live once you retire. You'll no longer be bound to living close to where you work. Your loved ones might live somewhere else, and retirement might be an opportunity to move closer to them. For some, they may be children, grandchildren, or other family members; for others, they may be close friends to eat cheesecake with during retirement. (Shout-out to *The Golden Girls*!) And realistically, some of us may not have people to plan retirement with—a much more common occurrence than we might think. In her book, *The Other Significant Others*, Rhaina Cohen (2024) explains:

> [Younger generations] are having fewer children, if they have children at all. This, in combination with marriage trends, has increased the number of older adults with no close family ties—a group of people whom sociologists call "elder orphans,' "solo agers," or "kinless." (p. 194)

In this case, planning for retirement may focus more on researching ready-made communities to become a part of or creating the kind of community you want at the last stages of life to bridge this gap.

Depending on your financial situation, investing in a new home might be a desirable option. Retirement might also be an opportunity to finally move to that place that is smaller or larger and in a geographic area that is warmer, colder, cheaper, or less crowded. Or it might be your chance to think about that place you once visited and fell in love with.

You don't have to make the big decision to move to a new place all at once. You can always have a trial period: Rent a place in that location for a few months. Of course, retirement might instead be your opportunity to stay put and enjoy where you live and the community that you have built, *without* having to go in to work each day. Regardless, take some time to dream a bit.

Planning Your Retirement Party

Perhaps you are someone who loves a party (especially when it's yours), and the idea of a retirement party is very exciting. Or maybe you're someone who is wanting to slip out quietly with no fuss, and the thought of a dozen other people focusing on you is uncomfortable.

While there are a lot of directions we could go in this section, we're just going to say it: Have a party! It can be just a few people at your favorite restaurant or hangout, or it can be many, many people in a large location.

Here are great reasons you should have a retirement party.

- **It's an opportunity to have people say nice things about the impact you've had on their lives and on the teaching profession:** It's possible that the next time people gather to say nice things about you will be your funeral. Of course, depending on your beliefs, you either will or won't be able to hear what they say about you at your funeral, so why not grab the opportunity to hear them when you retire?
- **It impacts your family, friends, and colleagues:** When other people gather to celebrate you and the work you have devoted much of your life to, the impact has a ripple effect on so many levels. If your family and friends are there, they will hear stories and comments about you that they've never heard, and they will understand you on a deeper level. Younger colleagues who are there will see their own possible career trajectory and reaffirm their belief that the work they are doing is important, valid, and life-changing. This can help them stay motivated as their years progress.
- **It can help you find closure:** As mentioned, your identity is going to shift when you retire. Just as a wedding, graduation ceremony, or birthday helps us transition from one chapter of our lives to another, a retirement party can help you transition to your next adventure. While we often discount the importance of ceremonies or other rites of passage, they mark many of the important moments and changes in our lives. We can't discount them:

> Without slowing down to give our transitions the sacred attention and respect they deserve, individuals may be challenged to find meaning in their life transitions. The lack of such rituals can lead to feelings of disconnection from self and others, anxiety, and even existential crisis. (Loupy, 2024)

The party doesn't mean you are finished working; it just means you're "graduating" from that job!

Reflections on the Journey: Gathering While You're Here

I had so much fun at my retirement party! It was incredible to have so many people from so many parts of my life come together to celebrate the work I'd done. I really loved hearing the stories about all of the memories people shared of us working together.

My wife actually is a celebrant for funerals. At funerals, the person [being celebrated] doesn't get to hear all of those stories, but at a retirement party, they do! And I took those stories into the next phase of my life. I knew that retirement didn't mean I wouldn't be working anymore or that I'd stop being productive. In my mind, the central focus of my retirement was how I could continue to be productive in other people's lives. (S. Bruecker, personal communication, November 1, 2025)

—Steve Bruecker
Physical education teacher

Strategies for Success: Plan Your Retirement Celebration

Following are a few tips for planning your retirement party or gathering.

- Choose a great emcee—someone who can keep things moving and the energy level high for the attendees. Of course, you might substitute this suggestion with "Choose a place with food you love and a nice private space" if you're having a smaller celebration.
- Ask the event emcee or planner to give a time limit for people who are going to share (and to make sure they stick to it). If you allot five minutes per person, but the first speaker goes for twenty minutes, people start to get uncomfortable and less interested. If there are no plans to have people speak, each of them could write a note with a memory or wish for you.
- Don't only invite the people you are currently working with. Invite people from all the different locations and phases of your career.

Final Thoughts

Whether you're looking forward to or dreading retirement—or feeling somewhere in between at any given moment—you've got this. There's a lot to think about financially, practically, and emotionally, but *you've got this*. Now you have a book of tools and resources to help you begin planning the important domains of your well-being in this final stage of your teaching career. This chapter attempts to empower you to make the choices and changes you can *now* to set yourself up as well as possible.

Remember, it's never too early to start!

Benefits Contact Questions

When will I be eligible to retire with full benefits?

How much pension will I receive each month?

How do those numbers change if I decide to retire before or after that?

What are the survivor benefits for my spouse/partner/dependents?

What happens with my health insurance? What about dental and vision insurance?

Does anything change with my benefits if I move out of my state or province?

Can I work part- or full-time *in my district* after I retire?

Can I work part- or full-time *outside my district* after I retire?

What happens with my unused sick and vacation days?

Are there options for increasing the amount I'm saving for retirement?

Does the district offer any retirement planning workshops or seminars?

When do I need to give my official notice of retirement, and what paperwork do I need to fill out?

Financial Experts

It's time to start planning for how you'll build your retirement dream team. If you haven't hired professionals for these roles, begin asking already-retired colleagues, friends, and family members for trusted recommendations and making appointments.

Role	Name	Contact
Financial adviser		
Tax specialist		
Estate specialist or attorney		
Health insurance adviser		
District representative you can go to with questions		

Final Thoughts on Your Grand Finale

We are your symphony, Mr. Holland. We are the melodies and the notes of your opus. We are the music of your life.

—Gertrude Lang

This classic line from *Mr. Holland's Opus*, a movie about a music teacher, brings a tear every time. We are aware that you didn't become a teacher with the consideration of your legacy first and foremost—yet here you are, heading toward the end of your run. And if you took a moment to reflect, you'd see the impact you have had on so many lives—students, colleagues, parents, and guardians chief among them.

In chapter 5, we spoke of how the one who plants the tree rarely gets to enjoy its shade. When we think about legacy, it's borne out of the notion that you chose to plant trees. You can't plant a tree without having some belief in the future. That's your legacy! A teacher's focus is not on creating good kindergarten students or good third-, seventh-, or eleventh-grade students. It's on creating good adults—people who can make positive, valuable, and viable contributions to their communities.

A Teaching Legacy

A teaching legacy means you might be the teacher who thrives on finding innovative strategies and methods for improving learning and assessment. You may be someone who thinks deeply and differently in areas related to behavior management or assessment, and your legacy might extend to writing to convey ideas, creating policies, or leading workshops. Some teachers' legacies come in the form of seeing a problem and creating a unique solution that they share with others. Your teaching legacy could impact your school, your district, or even the profession at large. Ultimately, your legacy is the sum of the personal and professional values, accomplishments, and actions that resonate with the people around you. It's how you have made a difference in the world.

Reflections on a Legacy

As this book draws to a close, we want you to reflect on your legacy. We start with a few questions originally adapted from *The Pedagogy of Confidence* (Jackson, 2011) for *Starting a Movement* (Williams & Hierck, 2015). Honestly consider each of the following questions about the journey you chose. Record your thoughts in the space provided.

What made you feel you had something to offer students to help them learn?

Remember your first year of teaching and the hope and desire you had to reach students. What did that motivate you to do?

What was your first piece of concrete evidence of your success in your teaching? How did it influence your passion and embolden you to use your gifts to unlock those of your students? What were the aptitudes or talents you acted on?

Think back to the students you had the most profound impact on. How did you engage them?

What did it feel like when you realized you had, in fact, made an impact?

The Forest You Grew

Many of this book's readers will have spent their entire careers in the same community—possibly in the same school. Some of our colleagues even attended the school where they teach. While we referenced planting trees whose shade you might not experience, we also know the following scenario to be true.

> *As I (Tom) move toward the end of my teacher career and walk the streets of my town or engage in the frivolities of social media, I am reminded of the "forest" I helped cultivate. I look up and see my "Sean tree" working in the local police station, my "Anna tree" teaching in another community, my "Gord tree" playing lead trombone in a big city symphony, my "Jenn tree" working as an administrative assistant, and so many others, both close to home and spread far from it. It's not just the trees' shade I enjoy but the brilliance of the light that shines through each of them. Not every one of their journeys was easy, and some didn't grow immediately tall and strong, but they all arrived in a place they were meant to be.*

You really have made a difference in the lives of so many—and not just your students'! Your students' children and partners also may join in the praise, since impact ripples out. Many of your colleagues will sing your praises and thank you for the work you did and the support you gave. The legend of Johnny Appleseed might be familiar to you. Johnny Appleseed roamed the frontier in ragged clothing, planting apple orchards. Perhaps it is time for a new legend? Let's imagine the legend of Jenny Bookseed, who planted the seeds of knowledge and nurtured the futures of so many.

References and Resources

Alboher, M. (2024, June 11). Why age diversity is a strength at work. *Greater Good Magazine*. Accessed at https://greatergood.berkeley.edu/article/item/why_age_diversity_is_a_strength_at_work on December 22, 2025.

Albulescu, P., Macsinga, I., Rusu, A., Sulea, C., Bodnaru, A., & Tulbure, B. T. (2022). "Give me a break!" A systematic review and meta-analysis on the efficacy of micro-breaks for increasing well-being and performance. *PLoS One, 17*(8), Article e0272460. https://doi.org/10.1371/journal.pone.0272460

Aldridge, E., & Witherspoon, M. G. (2023). Veteran teachers' resistance factors to technology usage in the face of change in the secondary classroom in northwest Alabama. *Alabama Journal of Educational Leadership, 10*, 99–116.

Alhajri, N., Hodges, N. J., Zwicker, J. G., & Virji-Babul, N. (*2018*). Mu suppression is sensitive to observational practice but results in different patterns of activation in comparison with physical practice. *Neural Plasticity*, 2018, Article 8309483. https://doi.org/10.1155/2018/8309483

Atchley, R. C. (1976). *The sociology of retirement*. Schenkman.

Bahns, A. J., Crandall, C. S., Gillath, O., & Preacher, K. J. (2017). Similarity in relationships as niche construction: Choice, stability, and influence within dyads in a free choice environment. *Journal of Personality and Social Psychology, 112*(2), 329–355. https://doi.org/10.1037/pspp0000088

Berhanu, K. Z. (2025). The relationship between principals' pedagogical leadership practices and teachers' job performance: The role of sociodemographic characteristics. *BMC Psychology, 13*, Article 89. https://doi.org/10.1186/s40359-025-02415-7

Berkeley Executive Education. (n.d.). *The importance of connections on our well-being* [Blog post]. Accessed at https://executive.berkeley.edu/thought-leadership/blog/importance-connections-our-well-being on December 18, 2025.

Blanchard, G. T. (2022, July 25). *The neuroscience of negative thinking* [Blog post]. Accessed at www.geralblanchard.com/the-neuroscience-of-negative-thinking on March 19, 2026.

Blazar, D., & Kraft, M. A. (2017). Teacher and teaching effects on students' attitudes and behaviors. *Educational Evaluation and Policy Analysis, 39*(1), 146–170. https://doi.org/10.3102/0162373716670260

Bone, J. K., Bu, F., Fluharty, M. E., Paul, E., Sonke, J. K., & Fancourt, D. (2022). Engagement in leisure activities and depression in older adults in the United States: Longitudinal evidence from the Health and Retirement Study. *Social Science and Medicine, 294*, Article 114703. https://doi.org/10.1016/j.socscimed.2022.114703

Boogren, T. H. (2025). *180 days of physical wellness for busy educators.* Solution Tree Press.

Business Wire. (2024, March 13). *MassMutual research: Most retirees are happier in retirement vs. working thanks to financial preparation, but more than one third report feeling lonely.* Business Wire. Accessed at www.businesswire.com/news/home/20240313372962/en/MassMutual-Research-Most-Retirees-are-Happier-in-Retirement-vs.-Working-Thanks-to-Financial-Preparation-but-More-than-One-Third-Report-Feeling-Lonely on April 1, 2026.

Campillo, I., Nunes, G., & Puertas, I. (2023, March 15). *Defining impact: A shift in thinking, acting and being.* Times Higher Education. Accessed at www.timeshighereducation.com/campus/defining-impact-shift-thinking-acting-and-being on October 23, 2025.

Chaiken, J., & Bierly, E. [@shrinkchicks]. (2025, December 17). *How to hold space for someone else without making it about you: From two licensed therapists* [Carousel post]. Instagram. Accessed at www.instagram.com/p/DSYhFGBDXeK/?img_index=1 on March 5, 2026.

City National Bank. (n.d.). *The hidden costs of retirement.* Accessed at www.cnb.com/personal-banking/insights/retirement-budgeting.html on September 22, 2025.

Clark, R. (2003). *The essential 55: An award-winning educator's rules for discovering the successful student in every child.* Hyperion.

Cohen, R. (2024). *The* other *significant others: Reimagining life with friendship at the center.* St. Martin's Press.

Collamer, N. (2013). *Second-act careers: 50+ ways to profit from your passions during semi-retirement.* Ten Speed Press.

Connelly, C. E., Černe, M., Dysvik, A., & Škerlavaj, M. (2019). Understanding knowledge hiding in organizations. *Journal of Organizational Behavior, 40*(7), 779–782.

Coristine, S., Russo, S., Fitzmorris, R., Beninato, P., & Rivolta, G. (2022). The importance of student-teacher relationships. In C. Vanner (Ed.), *Classroom practice in 2022.* University of Windsor. Accessed at https://ecampusontario.pressbooks.pub/educ5202/chapter/the-importance-of-student-teacher-relationships on May 20, 2025.

Cousineau, L. S., & Misener, K. (2019). Volunteering as meaning-making in the transition to retirement. *Canadian Journal of Nonprofit and Social Economy Research, 10*(1), 61–77.

Creative Leadership Solutions. (n.d.). *Changing the system.* Accessed at www.creativeleadership.net/resources-content/changing-the-system on October 24, 2025.

Day, C. (2012). New lives of teachers. *Teacher Education Quarterly, 39*(1), 7–26.

DeWitt, P. M., & Nelson, M. (2026). *Lead collectively: From belief to action to impact.* Corwin.

Diliberti, M. K., & Schwartz, H. L. (2025). *Educator turnover continues decline toward prepandemic levels: Findings from the American School District Panel (Report No. RR-A956-29). RAND.* Accessed at www.rand.org/pubs/research_reports/RRA956-29.html on September 22, 2025.

Dwyer, M., & Laird, E. (2024). *Up in the air: Educators juggling the potential of generative AI with detection, discipline, and distrust.* Center for Democracy & Technology. Accessed at https://cdt.org/wp-content/uploads/2024/03/2024-03-21-CDT-Civic-Tech-Generative-AI-Survey-Research-final.pdf on March 3, 2026.

Eller, J. F., & Hierck, T. (2021). *Trauma-sensitive instruction: Creating a safe and predictable classroom environment.* Solution Tree Press.

EXTRAordinary. (n.d.). *Chinese proverb: The best time to plant a tree was 20 years ago. The second best time is now [Blog post].* Accessed at www.extraordinary.live/blog-1-1/blog-post-onegodslove-s9t4h-7cc4z on March 31, 2026.

Fantilli, R. D., & McDougall, D. E. (2009). A study of novice teachers: Challenges and supports in the first years. *Teaching and Teacher Education, 25*(6), 814–825.

Ferlazzo, L. (2025, June 19). *How to change teachers' minds about leaving the classroom* [Blog post]. Accessed at www.edweek.org/teaching-learning/opinion-how-to-change-teachers-minds-about-leaving-the-classroom/2025/06 on October 23, 2025.

Fitzsimmons, F. (2023, August 29). *Mastering communication with Generation Z and Generation Alpha students [Blog post].* Accessed at www.keg.com/news/mastering-communication-with-generation-z-and-generation-alpha-students on March 19, 2026.

Fuchsman, D., McGee, J. B., & Zamarro, G. (2024). Teachers' knowledge and preparedness for retirement: Results from a nationally representative teacher survey. *AERA Open, 10*(1), 1–26. https://doi.org/10.1177/23328584241253819

Fullan, M. (1997). Emotion and hope: Constructive concepts for complex times. In A. Hargreaves (Ed.), *Rethinking educational change with heart and mind: 1997 ASCD yearbook* (pp. 216–233). ASCD.

Gallup. (2025). *State of the global workplace: Understanding employees, informing leaders.* Author. Accessed at https://healthyworkcompany.com/wp-content/uploads/2025/05/state-of-the-global-workplace-2025-download.pdf on June 17, 2026.

Gill, S. (2024, December 29). *How to catch and curb your complaining habit.* Katie Couric Media. Accessed at https://katiecouric.com/health/mental-health/how-to-stop-complaining on December 23, 2025.

Gladwell, M. (2008). *Outliers: The story of success.* Little, Brown.

Goodreads. (n.d.). *Anonymous Greek proverb quotes.* Accessed at www.goodreads.com/quotes/666987-society-grows-great-when-old-men-plant-trees-whose-shade on March 31, 2026.

Grant, A. (2013). *Give and take: A revolutionary approach to success.* Viking.

Gu, Q. (2017, June 20). *Relationships matter! Fostering and sustaining resilient teachers.* Teaching Times. Accessed at www.teachingtimes.com/pdt192-relationships-matter on December 22, 2025.

Haiilo. (2024, December 23). *Millennials in the workplace: 11 ways to attract and keep them* [Blog post]. Accessed at https://blog.haiilo.com/blog/millennials-in-the-workplace-11-ways-to-attract-and-keep-them on March 19, 2026.

Hardy, B. (2019, January 17). *Accountability partners are great. But "success" partners will change your life.* Medium. Accessed at https://medium.com/@benjaminhardy/accountability-partners-are-great-but-success-partners-will-change-your-life-8850ac0efa04 on March 2, 2026.

Herek, S. (Director). (1995). *Mr. Holland's opus* [Film]. Hollywood Pictures; Interscope Communications; PolyGram Filmed Entertainment.

Hierck, T. (2012a, January 27). *Tenet #9—If we don't model what we teach, then we are teaching what we model* [Blog post]. Accessed at https://umakeadiff.blogspot.com/2012/01/tenet-9-if-we-dont-model-what-we-teach.html on December 19, 2025.

Hierck, T. (2012b, January 30). *Tenet #10—First with the heart, then with the head* [Blog post]. Accessed at https://umakeadiff.blogspot.com/2012_01_01_archive.html on December 19, 2025.

Hierck, T., & Kajitani, A. (2024). *You're a teacher now! What's next?* Solution Tree Press.

Huang, K., Yeomans, M., Brooks, A. W., Minson, J., & Gino, F. (2017). It doesn't hurt to ask: Question-asking increases liking. *Journal of Personality and Social Psychology, 113*(3), 430–452. https://doi.org/10.1037/pspi0000097

Jackson, S. (2024, January 11). *Sam Altman says it's 'potentially a little scary' how quickly society will have to adapt to the AI revolution.* Business Insider. Accessed at www.businessinsider.com/sam-altman-ai-revolution-requires-society-adapt-faster-than-ever-2024-1 on October 14, 2025.

Jackson, Y. (2011). *The pedagogy of confidence: Inspiring high intellectual performance in urban schools.* Teachers College Press.

Jeffery, R. (2023, August 8). *Transitioning from work/life balance to retirement/life balance.* Alberta Retired Teachers' Association. Accessed at www.arta.net/living-well/mental-health/retire-refire-rewire-harmony-in-retirement on December 26, 2025.

John Hancock & MIT AgeLab. (2025). *Longevity Preparedness Index: How prepared are US adults for living longer, healthier,* better *lives?* Authors. Accessed at www.johnhancock.com/content/dam/onejohnhancock/pdfs/longevity-preparedness-index/life-4231-longevity-preparedness-index-facts-and-findings.pdf on February 4, 2026.

Kajitani, A. (2016, August 22). Another year, another principal: How to manage your relationship with a new principal for the good of your school. *Education Week.* Accessed at www.edweek.org/teaching-learning/opinion-another-year-another-principal-how-to-manage-your-relationship-with-a-new-principal-for-the-good-of-your-school/2016/08 on March 30, 2026.

Kajitani, A. (2022). *101 tips for teaching online: Helping students think, learn, and grow—no matter where they are!* Solution Tree Press.

Kets de Vries, M. F. R. (2023, July/August). Why it's so hard to ask for help. *Harvard Business Review*. Accessed at https://hbr.org/2023/07/why-its-so-hard-to-ask-for-help on June 8, 2025.

Kircher, M. M., & Holtermann, C. (2026, February 26). A blow to the phone-free classroom. *The New York Times*. Accessed at www.nytimes.com/2026/02/25/style/yondr-pouch-school-phone-ban.html on March 3, 2026.

Kofke, D. (2026). *Where to spend, where to save: A teacher's guide to managing your finances*. Solution Tree Press.

Kreuzfeld, S., & Seibt, R. (2024). Work ability and psychosocial work stress—Predictors of retirement intention among older teachers. *International Journal of Occupational Medicine and Environmental Health, 37*(5), 508–523. https://doi.org/10.13075/ijomeh.1896.02454

Lachman, M. E., Lipsitz, L., Lubben, J., Castaneda-Sceppa, C., & Jette, A. M. (2018). When adults don't exercise: Behavioral strategies to increase physical activity in sedentary middle-aged and older adults. *Innovation in Aging, 2*(1), Article igy007. https://doi.org/10.1093/geroni/igy007

LaRue, L. A. N. (2022, February 9–12). *When retirement calls: Preparing to thrive* [Conference presentation]. Association of Presbyterian Church Educators Annual Event, Chicago, IL, United States.

Lee, H. (2022, November 17). *The changing generational values: Examining workplace values from Baby Boomers to Generation Z* [Blog post]. Accessed at https://imagine.jhu.edu/blog/2022/11/17/the-changing-generational-values on March 19, 2026.

Lodwick, A. (2023, April 26). *Asking for help from colleagues the right way (and why you should)* [Blog post]. Accessed at https://reviewstudio.com/blog/asking-for-help-from-colleagues-the-right-way-and-why-you-should on February 4, 2026.

Loewus, L. (2021, May 4). Why teachers leave—or don't: A look at the numbers. *Education Week*. Accessed at www.edweek.org/teaching-learning/why-teachers-leave-or-dont-a-look-at-the-numbers/2021/05 on May 22, 2025.

Loupy, K. (2024, December 23). *Lost in transition: How reviving rites of passage might support mental health—part 1 of 2* [Blog post]. Accessed at https://psychiatryinstitute.com/lost-in-transition-how-reviving-rites-of-passage-might-support-mental-health-part-1-of-2 on March 19, 2026.

Luo, P., Liu, Y., Pan, X., & Huang, L. (2024). Mental health status and influencing factors of retired teachers. *Frontiers in Public Health, 12*, Article 1358285. https://doi.org/10.3389/fpubh.2024.1358285

MacLean, M. B., Wolfson, C., Hewko, S., Tompa, E., Sweet, J., & Pedlar, D. (2025). Predictors of retirement voluntariness using Canadian longitudinal study on aging data. *Journal of Aging and Health, 37*(1–2), 75–95.

MassMutual & PBS Insights. (2024). *2024 MassMutual retirement happiness study*. Authors. Accessed at www.massmutual.com/global/media/shared/doc/2024_massmutual_retirement_happiness_study.pdf on April 2, 2026.

Matthews, K., & Nazroo, J. (2021). The impact of volunteering and its characteristics on well-being after state pension age: Longitudinal evidence from the English Longitudinal Study of Ageing. *The Journals of Gerontology: Series B—Psychological Sciences and Social Sciences, 76*(3), 632–641. https://doi.org/10.1093/geronb/gbaa146

McDowell, M. (2021, April 14). *3 ways experienced teachers can get more out of professional development*. Edutopia. Accessed at www.edutopia.org/article/3-ways-experienced-teachers-can-get-more-out-professional-development on October 23, 2025.

Meltzer, E. (2025, October 20). *A new study confirms a hunch: School cellphone bans can boost test scores*. Chalkbeat. Accessed at www.chalkbeat.org/2025/10/20/new-study-finds-cell-phone-ban-benefits-to-test-scores on March 3, 2026.

Mohammed, J. (2025, May). *Why preparing emotionally for retirement is just as important as having a financial plan*. Maclean's. Accessed at https://macleans.ca/society/preparing-emotionally-for-retirement-is-important on December 12, 2025.

National Institute on Aging. (2024, June 11). *Cognitive health and older adults*. Accessed at www.nia.nih.gov/health/brain-health/cognitive-health-and-older-adults on February 4, 2026.

Newberg, A., & Waldman, M. R. (2012). *Words can change your brain: 12 conversation strategies to build trust, resolve conflict, and increase intimacy*. Hudson Street Press.

Newman, K. M. (2025, July 30). How does retirement affect our health and happiness? *Greater Good Magazine*. Accessed at https://greatergood.berkeley.edu/article/item/how_does_retirement_affect_our_health_and_happiness on February 4, 2026.

NordForsk. (2025, March 2). *Inclusive school environments begin with knowledge sharing and collaboration*. Accessed at www.nordforsk.org/news/inclusive-school-environments-begin-knowledge-sharing-and-collaboration on March 2, 2026.

Nurenberg, D., & Tuller, L. (2023). "All in this together": Improving access to accelerated learning through embedding honors in heterogeneously grouped classes. *Teachers College Record: The Voice of Scholarship in Education, 125*(9), 3–50.

Ong, A. D., Mann, F. D., & Kubzansky, L. D. (2025). Cumulative social advantage is associated with slower epigenetic aging and lower systemic inflammation. *Brain, Behavior, and Immunity—Health, 48*, Article 101096. https://doi.org/10.1016/j.bbih.2025.101096

Papert, S. (1998, June 2). *Child power: Keys to the new learning of the digital century* [Speech]. 11th Colin Cherry Memorial Lecture on Communication, London, England.

Parkin, G., & Winsborough, D. (2025, July 20). From corner office to crossroads: Navigating purpose and identity after retirement. *The Guardian*. Accessed at www.theguardian.com/commentisfree/2025/jul/21/from-corner-office-to-crossroads-navigating-purpose-and-identity-after-retirement on April 2, 2026.

Patterson, A. (2025, June 3). *Colleagues in conflict? How to defuse workplace disagreements.* University of Auckland. Accessed at www.auckland.ac.nz/en/news/2025/06/03/seven-tips-to-defuse-workplace-disagreements.html on March 19, 2026.

Perry, A. (2025, February 19). You can't solve the teacher shortage by pretending anyone can do the job. *The Walrus.* Accessed at https://thewalrus.ca/you-cant-solve-the-teacher-shortage-by-pretending-anyone-can-do-the-job on March 5, 2026.

Pilehvari, A., You, W., & Lin, X. (2023). Retirement's impact on health: What role does social network play? *European Journal of Ageing, 20,* Article 14. https://doi.org/10.1007/s10433-023-00759-w

Podolsky, A., Kini, T., Bishop, J., & Darling-Hammond, L. (2016). *Solving the teacher shortage: How to attract and retain excellent educators.* Learning Policy Institute. Accessed at https://learningpolicyinstitute.org/media/180/download?inline&file=Solving_Teacher_Shortage_Attract_Retain_Educators_REPORT.pdf on April 3, 2026.

Potdar, M. (2023, June 5). *Institutional memory: Preserving organisational knowledge for success.* LinkedIn. Accessed at www.linkedin.com/pulse/institutional-memory-preserving-organisational-knowledge-mayur-potdar on October 15, 2025.

Prothero, A. (2023, April 20). Student behavior isn't getting any better, survey shows. *Education Week.* Accessed at www.edweek.org/leadership/student-behavior-isnt-getting-any-better-survey-shows/2023/04 on February 4, 2026.

Quintet, J. (2025, May 1). *Quebec to ban cellphones in all schools—Here's what that means.* iPhone in Canada. Accessed at www.iphoneincanada.ca/2025/05/01/quebec-to-ban-cellphones-in-all-schools-heres-what-that-means on March 3, 2026.

Ryan, R. M., & Deci, E. L. (2000). Self-determination theory and the facilitation of intrinsic motivation, social development, and well-being. *American Psychologist, 55*(1), 68–78.

Sanderse, W. (2024). The intersection of teacher modelling and student emulation in moral education. *On Education: Journal for Research and Debate, 7*(19).

Schroeder, J. (2024, June 4). How to overcome identity loss in retirement. *Kiplinger.* Accessed at www.kiplinger.com/retirement/how-to-overcome-identity-loss-in-retirement on September 22, 2025.

Tariq, B., Dilawar, M., & Muhammad, Y. (2019). Innovative teaching and technology integration: Exploring elderly teachers' attitudes. *International Journal of Distance Education and E-Learning, 5*(1). https://doi.org/10.36261/ijdeel.v5i1.789

threefold consulting. (2015, November 23). *Otto Scharmer on the four levels of listening* [Video file]. Accessed at www.youtube.com/watch?v=eLfXpRkVZaI on November 19, 2025.

Toubiana, M., Ruebottom, T., & Hakak, L. T. (2022, January 28). When a major life change upends your sense of self. *Harvard Business Review.* Accessed at https://hbr.org/2022/01/when-a-major-life-change-upends-your-sense-of-self on April 2, 2026.

Troen, V., & Boles, K. C. (2012). *The power of teacher teams: With cases, analyses, and strategies for success.* Corwin.

U2. (2000). Stuck in a moment you can't get out of [Song]. On *All that you can't leave behind.* Island Records; Interscope Records.

Vo, T. T., & Phu-Duyen, T. T. (2023). Mental health around retirement: Evidence of Ashenfelter's dip. *Global Health Research and Policy, 8,* Article 35. https://doi.org/10.1186/s41256-023-00320-3

Vygotsky, L. S. (1978). *Mind in society: The development of higher psychological processes* (M. Cole, V. John-Steiner, S. Scribner, & E. Souberman, Eds.). Harvard University Press.

Wagner, G. D. (2017, June 20). The importance of fitness buddies. *Experience Life.* Accessed at https://experiencelife.lifetime.life/article/strength-in-numbers-the-importance-of-fitness-buddies on March 2, 2026.

Whalen, C. (2025, May 29). *Running on empty: Teachers not prepared for increased challenging behaviors.* RethinkEd. Accessed at www.rethinked.com/resources/teachers-not-prepared-increasing
-challenging-behaviors on February 4, 2026.

White, M. (2022). *5-gen leadership: Leading 5 generations in schools in the 2020s.* Corwin.

Williams, K. C., & Hierck, T. (2015). *Starting a movement: Building culture from the inside out in professional learning communities.* Solution Tree Press.

Wolcott, G. (2019). *Significant 72: Unleashing the power of relationships in today's schools.* FIRST Educational Resources.

Wong, H. K., & Wong, R. T. (1998). *The first days of school: How to be an effective teacher* (2nd ed.). Wong.

Index

You're a Teacher Now! What's Next?
You're a Principal Now! What's Next?
In companion books *You're a Principal Now! What's Next?* and *You're a Teacher Now! What's Next?*, educators get an easy-to-reference FAQ approach that offers insight, strategies, and tools to new principals and teachers so they know more about the aspects of teaching that often go unacknowledged.
BKG309, BKG142

Joy!
Timothy D. Kanold
Renowned educator Timothy D. Kanold takes readers through a mindful reflection of joy's significance in one's personal and professional life. Drawing on cultural concepts, insightful narratives, and brain research, he illustrates the discovery and conscious pursuit of joy to encourage reconnection with hope, purpose, engagement, and life balance.
BKG258

Owning It
Alex Kajitani
Today's fast-changing culture presents a great challenge—and a great opportunity—in schools and in the teaching profession. With *Owning It*, you will discover an array of easy-to-implement strategies designed to help you excel in your classroom, at your school, and in your community.
BKF835

The Educator Wellness Plan Book and Journal
Tina H. Boogren, Timothy D. Kanold, and Jasmine K. Kullar
This plan book and journal serves as a companion guide to *Educator Wellness: A Guide for Sustaining Physical, Mental, Emotional, and Social Well-Being*. Prioritize four dimensions of wellness with weekly routines and reflection prompts to help you commit to wellness practices throughout the school year.
BKG139

Solution Tree | Press a division of Solution Tree

Visit SolutionTree.com or call 800.733.6786 to order.

We don't just help schools make a change, we help them ***be* the change**

REAL IMPACT. RELEVANT SOLUTIONS. RESULTS-DRIVEN APPROACH.

From funding to faculty retention, the evolving demands schools face can be overwhelming. That's where we come in. With professional development rooted in decades of research and delivered by many of the educators who literally wrote the book on it, we empower schools to achieve meaningful change with real, sustainable results.

The change starts here. We can make it happen together.

See how we can get real results for your school or district.

Scan the code or visit:

SolutionTree.com/Results-Driven

WE CAN!

Solution Tree

LET'S SEE WHAT **WE CAN** DO TOGETHER